D1566883

Lives of Mothers
& Daughters

Lives of Mothers & Daughters

Growing Up With Alice Munro

SHEILA MUNRO

National Library of Canada Cataloguing in Publication Data

Munro, Sheila, 1953-
    Lives of mothers and daughters: growing up with Alice Munro

Includes index.
ISBN 0-7710-6669-4

1. Munro, Alice, 1931- . 2. Munro, Sheila, 1953- . 3. Authors, Canadian (English) – 20th Century – Biography.* I. Title.

PS8576.U57Z78 2001   C813'.54   C00-932720-7
PR9199.3.M8Z78 2001

We acknowledge the financial support of the Government of Canada through the Book Publishing Industry Development Program for our publishing activities. We further acknowledge the support of the Canada Council for the Arts and the Ontario Arts Council for our publishing program.

Typeset in Minion by M&S, Toronto
Printed and bound in Canada

A Douglas Gibson Book

McClelland & Stewart Ltd.
The Canadian Publishers
481 University Avenue
Toronto, Ontario
M5G 2E9
www.mcclelland.com

1   2   3   4   5   05   04   03   02   01

For my mother and father

Tell all the Truth but tell it slant –
Success in Circuit lies
Too bright for our infirm Delight
The Truth's superb surprise
As Lightning to the Children eased
With explanation kind
The Truth must dazzle gradually
Or every man be blind –

Emily Dickinson

CONTENTS

CHAPTER 1

Engagement and Marriage
1949 –1951

NEWLYWEDS

I am looking at photographs of my parents taken in the early fifties soon after they were married, small black-and-white photographs taped onto the pages of a tattered green Scrap Album. Some of them are fading, others have starbursts of white shadows blooming on them. Here is my mother at Spanish Banks Beach in Vancouver posing obligingly in one of those structured bathing suits that have become popular again now that the baby boomers are aging, canting her hips so they won't look too wide, her long dark hair blowing in the wind. Here are my parents together that same day, my father looking lean and handsome, posing with his arm a little awkwardly around his young wife. It is obvious he enjoyed taking pictures of her. She is full-faced and full-figured, and has that small waist that was so highly prized in the fifties; with her pale skin, her dark lips, and her long hair, my mother is beautiful, with only a suggestion around the eyes (or am I imagining this?) that she is partly play-acting the role of happily married young housewife.

My father and mother at Kitsilano Beach, in Vancouver in 1952, with Stanley Park and the North Shore mountains in the background.

He took pictures of her around the sights of Vancouver: in front of the chairlift up on Grouse Mountain; at the Stanley Park Zoo with all the gloom of the Vancouver winter pressing in on her; on the Capilano Suspension Bridge, where she bravely grips the rail; and on the deck of the ferry, the "Princess Marguerite," on an overnight trip they took to Victoria, the city they would move to thirteen years later. There they are together again, posing with vulnerable formality in front of the Empress Hotel, my parents in their early twenties, poised on the brink of fifties domesticity, ready and even eager to take on the burdens and responsibilities ahead of them. There were none of these blurred edges between youth and maturity, none of this talk about having to find yourself that kept my generation in such a prolonged adolescence. That was the way it was then. You got married and plunged headlong into the serious business of adult life.

My mother and father in front of the Empress Hotel in Victoria, 1952.

ENGAGED

My parents met at the University of Western Ontario. Like the character Rose in the story "The Beggar Maid," published in Canada in the collection *Who Do You Think You Are?*, and unlike Del in *Lives of Girls and Women*, who fails to win the scholarship because her brain has been addled by sex, Alice Laidlaw did win a scholarship to go to university. On the grade-thirteen examinations she wrote in Wingham, she received the highest marks in Huron County, with firsts in English, History, Latin, French, Zoology, and Biology, and a second in German. In 1949, thinking it was more practical than English, and had more cachet ("It sounded more fashionable to tell people I was going into journalism"), she entered Western's new journalism program.

My father, Jim Munro, came from Oakville, Ontario, a lake-shore town just an hour west of Toronto. The only reason he was at the University of Western Ontario instead of the University of Toronto was that he had failed his grade-thirteen trigonometry exam, and entrance requirements at Western were less stringent than those at Toronto. (I often amuse myself by thinking about how I owe my existence to that trigonometry exam.) He studied History for two years before deciding to switch to the General Arts Program, where he could take more courses in English and Philosophy.

Alice and Jim met in the university library when he was in second year and she was in first year. Before they met he'd already had his eye on her; he told me, "I'd seen her around but I didn't know anything about her." One day they happened to be sitting across from each other in the library, studying. (I suspect he engineered things so he would be sitting across from her.) He was surreptitiously munching on some chocolate-covered candies when he dropped one on the floor. He was just looking down wondering whether to pick it up when Alice said, "I'll eat it."

Like Rose in "The Beggar Maid," as a scholarship student, my mother was usually half starved. She had breakfast at the boarding house where she lived and then had thirty-five cents to spend on food for the rest of the day. That meant she could have a sandwich, a cup of coffee, and sometimes a butter tart at a local coffee shop. That was all she could afford. Besides holding down two library jobs, again like Rose, she sold her blood as often as possible to make a little extra cash, but she still didn't have enough money to live on. During the day she would sit in the library studying until she couldn't think of anything besides food, so she was probably very hungry the day my father dropped the candy.

After that encounter Jim tried to find out more about her. "I remember asking who she was. Someone said, 'Oh, that's Alice Laidlaw, the *Folio*'s new find.'" *Folio* was Western's literary magazine, and by this time she had published the first of three stories she wrote for it: "Dimensions of a Shadow," which appeared in April of 1950. Following the candy incident, my father called her and she agreed to go out with him, even though she couldn't quite remember who he was. He told me he was "crazy about her" and the courtship proceeded at a dizzying pace. Six months later, before the summer break, they were engaged.

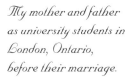

My mother and father as university students in London, Ontario, before their marriage.

FIRST STORIES

"Dimensions of a Shadow" is the sad story of Miss Abelhart, a spinster Latin teacher who ekes out an existence in a small Ontario town. She is only thirty-three but she has always been old: "There was no blood in her cheeks, and something like dust lay over her face." One evening in June Miss Abelhart comes out of church, daringly turns down an invitation to a temperance meeting, and goes for a walk by herself. "The sky was hidden in pale soft clouds, promising rain, and the air was warm and still. The dusty, hurrying smells of the day were not in it, only the heavy sweetness of lilacs, already past their prime, and the rich scent of peonies." While she is walking, she enters into a daydream about a boy in her Latin class. She tries to stop herself: "I am making this up; it cannot be true." But it is too late and she slips across some invisible boundary and suddenly he appears to her on the street and the two of them walk together and the boy admits to his feelings for her. When she is saying goodbye to him we realize it has all been a fantasy. "She thought there was somebody right there beside her." Some girls have been watching her. After their laughter falls away, "Miss Abelhart was alone in a bottomless silence."

My mother submitted this story to a fellow undergraduate, Gerry Fremlin (who, more than twenty years later, was to become her second husband), under the mistaken impression that he was the editor of *Folio*. She thought of Gerry as something of a Byronic figure on campus, dark and lean, and a few years older than everyone else because he had been in the War, flying bombing missions over Germany and Japan. At Western he had entered the journalism program too, but switched to English and Philosophy, and finally took Geography by correspondence, earning two degrees over a period of eight years. He also wrote poetry for *Folio*.

Gerry remembers seeing the editor of *Folio* running down the hall after reading the story, waving it in his hand and shouting "You've got to read this. You've got to read this." Gerry did read the story, and he was so impressed he later wrote the author a letter comparing her to Chekhov, saying there were phrases of "great poetry" in her writing. He was not romantically attracted, however; to him she was "an apple-cheeked country girl" and he had other attachments. Besides, by the time he wrote the letter she was already engaged to my father, who had, in Gerry's words, "swooped down like an eagle and carried her off."

The summer after my parents were engaged, Alice worked as a waitress at the Milford Manor resort in Muskoka, the lake-and-woods country north of Toronto. It was here that she received the letter from Gerald Fremlin comparing her to Chekhov. Others had noticed her talent, too. Looking back on his days at Western, fellow undergraduate and future English professor Douglas Spettigue remembered her quiet determination. "She was shy and small and had a very white face. . . . She calls one of her heroines 'commonplace pretty.' Alice was not commonplace pretty but you expected her to be. You thought you could stare right through those quiet eyes and the girl would disappear. But she didn't. There was an unexpected strength there, and even then a confidence that some of the rest of us, noisier, may have envied. We knew that she was writing, but then everyone was writing."

Back in London for her second year at Western, she was persuaded to switch from Journalism to the English program. "I was corralled by the English professors," she told me, and that year she took courses in Drama, Aesthetics, Medieval History, French Literature, and Latin, while continuing to write stories.

By then she was in with my father's arty theatre crowd at Western, the group who were involved in the Players' Guild and the Hesperian Club, as well as writing for *Folio*. Spettigue noted that once again "Alice seems to me to have been on the edge of the group. Perhaps she was less in circulation because already Jim Munro was on the scene; I remember being told that Alice 'had her ring,' and she was married in 1951 when she was only twenty." Whether she was on the fringes or not, she did write an adaptation of Ibsen's *Peer Gynt* (a play usually regarded as very hard to perform on stage) for a production put on by the Players' Guild, which was by all accounts a great success.

That spring she and my father attended a literary evening hosted by a young professor, where she read one of her stories, "The Man Who Goes Home," about a man who takes the train home to the town he is from, and who for some reason, some unaccountable nostalgia, can't bear to see the town the way it is now, and simply waits at the station until the next train back. While she was reading, she was surprised to look up and see Gerry in the crowd. By this time he was driving a taxi in London and she had lost track of him. After she finished the story, he raised his hand and asked her why she hadn't called the town Wingham (she called it Maitland). A little flustered, she managed to say something about not using real names in fiction, and the chance encounter was soon forgotten.

During that year she published two more stories in *Folio.* "Story for Sunday," in the December 1950 issue, and "The Widower" in April of 1951. In "Story for Sunday," a young girl, Evelyn, becomes infatuated with the new Sunday school super-intendent, the mysterious Mr. Willens, after he speaks kindly to her and kisses her one Sunday, in a little room by the church vestry. She spends the next week in a kind of ecstatic reverie ("the glow of the secret trembled inside her"), convinced that he loves her, even though she is "a lumpish thing," big and clumsy and not feminine like Myrtle Fotheringay, who plays the piano in church. The next Sunday she is on her way to the vestry to see him again when she overhears him murmuring the same words to Myrtle Fotheringay, and sees him kissing her. Somehow she manages to get down the stairs and finds a hymn book open in her hand, and she begins singing "Thou O Christ, art all I want," and as she is singing she discovers something "greater than a mean little private love, more strange and wonderful. . . ." She experiences a curious epiphany when she looks up from the hymn book to find the face of Mr. Willens has merged with the image of the "immaculate Christ."

"The Widower" explores the inner life of a retired grocer, Mr. McManus, after his wife has died. Not particularly sorry about his bereavement, he observes the funeral as if from a great distance and returns home to his wife's geraniums and African violets, and makes himself a cup of tea. He looks back on the claustrophobia of a life with a woman who bound herself to him tightly ("A woman was like that when she didn't have any children"), remembering the guilty pleasure he would feel when his wife was out at the Mission Circle and he would play his violin.

Now that she is gone, he imagines that some "free, lonely, happy life was about to begin for him." He goes for a walk and feels excited again by the dreams of his youthful self. "He would go away, he would wander about and see the old tall cities, the countries across the sea; he would learn to play the violin as he wanted to play; he would buy a farm like the farm he remembered. . . ." But then he realizes it is too late, he is much too old, his wife "might as well not be dead." A neighbour peeks through her curtains at him trudging home and we hear that unmistakable Munro irony, the way the conventional view of things is so far from the truth. "*He's going home*, she would say to her husband. *He just sits at home all by himself, he's that lost without his wife.*"

THE BEGGAR MAID

When I try to imagine my parents' courtship, scenes from the story "The Beggar Maid" roll through my mind like reels from a movie I have seen, a movie in which my mother stars as Rose, the poor scholarship student, while my father stars as Patrick, the wealthy department-store heir. I see the other scholarship girls with their "meekly smiling gratitude, their large teeth and maidenly rolls of hair," and my mother defiantly wearing tarty clothes. I see my father looking scornful when someone mispronounces the name Metternich, just as Patrick looks. I picture him waiting outside my mother's boarding house in the snow, so vulnerable, so in love.

When Patrick visits Rose's family I see my father sitting at the kitchen table at my mother's house at the end of Lowertown Road in Wingham and seeing the plastic swan with the paper napkins in it and my mother being ashamed on more levels than she can count. When Rose visits Patrick's family I see my grandparents' massive dining-room table in Oakville and feel the weight of the heavy silverware, just as Rose does, and also feel the childish belligerence that Rose describes, and I pass judgement on them as if this is the way they really were. Rose's attempt to break her engagement, and the self-betrayal and vanity in her capitulation to her need to make Patrick happy, her need to be worshipped, all of this makes me feel as though I have entered into my mother's psyche, that these are her own feelings about her marriage.

I know I am on dangerous ground here. I tell myself I am wrong to see fiction in this way, that fiction, even autobiographical fiction, is not the same as autobiography, but I can't change it, I can't unravel the truth of my mother's fiction from the reality of what actually happened. So much of what I think I know, and I think I know more about my mother's life than almost any daughter could know, is refracted through the prism of her writing. So unassailable is the truth of her fiction that sometimes I even feel as though I'm living inside an Alice Munro story. It's as if her view of the world must be the way the world really is, because it feels so convincing, so true, that you trust her every word.

My mother visiting my father's family in Oakville in 1951, two months before the wedding. From left to right: Barb Munro, Arthur Munro (my grandfather), Margaret Munro (my grandmother), John Munro, my mother, my father, and Donald Dean.

WHY MARRIAGE?

I do know that my mother was happy to be engaged.
  "It was something I had to do. The whole thing about getting engaged and married was so totally appealing. You really didn't want to graduate from university."

It was the beginning of the fifties, that decade so notorious to later feminists, a time when the curious logic of Freudian thinking permeated the culture. Yes, it was good for a woman to be educated, according to this line of reasoning, more or less for the sake of her children and to be a credit to her husband, but a woman who became too educated put at risk her most precious commodity, femininity, and could become frigid, or even barren, as a result. Brainy, ambitious women, women who did not accept the passive role with good grace, suffered from a "masculinity complex" and were bound to be less attractive to men and likely to wind up old maids at twenty-five, cast off forever from the prospect of feminine fulfilment.

My mother cared about being sexually attractive and may have been a little insecure about whether she would pass this test (like the girl in "Red Dress – 1946" who doesn't get asked to dance until she has almost given up hope). She never had any intention of resisting marriage and motherhood. For her it was always a matter of *both/and*, rather than *either/or*. As a little girl she imagined how she would be a movie star *and* have quintuplets. "I was going to have five girls and they were all different, there was a blue-eyed blonde, a blue-eyed black-haired one, there was a green-eyed red-haired one, a brown-eyed blonde, and then there was a brunette. So I had all types and I had their names, all their clothes. I remember they all had reversible pleated skirts, which were very fashionable at the time."

She wanted a conventional life that included a husband and children, and beyond that she needed some kind of protective camouflage to conceal her raw ambition from the rest of the world. She could never have imagined going off to Paris and declaring herself a writer the way Mavis Gallant did. For her that would have been sheer folly, a dangerous exposure. I've heard writers and critics who marvel at my mother's ability to be a writer and the mother of three daughters. I know myself that the domestic life can combine very well with writing, if you can get some time alone. It offers both privacy and a kind of anonymity that allow you to sink down into your life and be an inconspicuous observer. It allows you to remain neutral to some degree, not to take any particular stance in your life, and that was what she needed. I don't think you can remain detached in the same way if you have a career that is at all demanding. Raising children also gives you experiences, it gives your life a structure and a shape, so you have something to write about, and it anchors you in reality.

My mother also counted herself lucky, very lucky, to have met a man who not only read books and appreciated literature, but understood and supported her need to be a serious writer. "Hardly any men of that generation were like that." For women to have those kind of aspirations, "to do something on the serious level that men worked on, of absolute seriousness, was unthinkable."

If she had been more popular in high school, if she had gone on dates (my mother did not have the kind of sexual experience that Del Jordan had in *Lives of Girls and Women*; even though she was pretty, boys sensed that there was something odd about her, and kept their distance), or if she hadn't won the scholarship, she could have wound up married to a farmer. She could see herself accepting a proposal, "and then where would I be? How could I possibly have found time to write as a farmer's wife?"

There were other pressures, other reasons as well, that made the prospect of an early marriage to my father irresistible. The scholarship only lasted for two years, so it would have been impossible for her to go back to university to complete her degree in any case. "When I was on the scholarship I had enough just to eat and pay my rent, and I worked at the library but I never saved anything, and so when the year came to an end I didn't have enough for anything except to go home. How could I have managed?" She thought of going to Toronto to look for work, but then she came up against the Catch-22 of what to live on while she was looking for a job. Perhaps she could have borrowed some money, "if I had been a more aggressive sort of person." If all else failed she could have applied for work at the glove factory in Wingham, but given her lack of manual dexterity, it was very likely she would have been fired. And underlying what were undeniably valid and legitimate reasons was something else, a subconscious holding-back from any kind of commitment that would sidetrack her writing.

After two years at Western, what was there to do but return to Wingham to help look after a mother bedridden with Parkinson's disease, a father who was a night watchman at the Wingham Foundry after the failure of his mink and fox farm, and a younger brother and sister still in their early teens? Home again in May of 1951, she "worked keeping house, terribly hard" (with one brief interval in the summer when she had a job removing the suckers from tobacco plants), until December of that year, when she married my father.

While my mother was keeping house in Wingham, my father spent the summer after graduating from Western in the navy "out west," stationed at Naden, near Victoria. Too young to be in the War, as he was only fifteen when it ended, my father had been in the naval reserve, the Cadet Corps, at university, and was taking courses at Royal Roads Military College. That summer he became so enamoured of the West Coast he decided that he and my mother should settle there. Rather than returning to Ontario, that fall he managed to land a job at the Eaton's store in Vancouver, where he worked until Christmas, before taking the train back to Ontario to marry my mother at her parents' home in Wingham on December 29, 1951. The notice in the Wingham paper read as follows:

The wedding of Alice Ann Laidlaw, Daughter of Mr. and Mrs. R.E. Laidlaw, of Wingham, and James Armstrong Munro, of Oakville took place at the home of the bride's parents. The ceremony was performed by Dr. W.A. Beecroft, of Wingham. Miss Diane Lane, of St. Thomas, played wedding music. Given in marriage by her father, the bride wore an afternoon dress of wine velvet with matching accessories and a corsage of

A wedding portrait of my parents with my mother's parents, on December 29, 1951.

Lester Hibbard roses. Miss Sheila Laidlaw was her sister's only attendant, wearing a dress of sapphire blue velvet matching accessories and a corsage of pink delight roses. Groomsman was Donald Dean, Tillsonburg. Following a wedding trip to Banff, Alta. Mr. and Mrs. Munro will make their home at Vancouver.

During the wedding service my mother started crying. She tried to reach for her handkerchief but my father wouldn't let go of her hand.

JIM MUNRO

The man Alice married came from a background about as different from hers as I could imagine. The eldest of four children, my father grew up in a gracious, ivy-covered home surrounded by an expanse of lawns and gardens just half a block from Lake Ontario in Oakville. He was not the heir to a chain of department stores like Patrick Blatchford in "The Beggar Maid," but his father, Arthur Munro, better known as "Pork," was a successful accountant who became the auditor for the Timothy Eaton Company in Toronto, almost an hour by car to the east. And in those days, working for Eaton's, the Canada-wide department-store chain, conferred immense status on any head office executive.

His mother, Margaret Armstrong, was a practical, literal-minded woman whose father had owned the tannery in Oakville when she was a girl. The Armstrongs were part of the local elite. They were one of the first families in town to own a car, chauffeur-driven, of course, and their home was a grand

Georgian mansion surrounded by verandahs. In the mid-twenties, the tannery suddenly went broke in mysterious circumstances and the family fortune was lost, but by that time Margaret was already grown up.

Jim Munro's sister Barbara was born only eighteen months after him; John and Margaret came along a few years later. The parents obviously favoured Barbara over her older brother, and the rivalry went very deep with him. Barbara was the practical one, the "smart" one who excelled at math. "Some day she's going to make more money than you," his father told him, a cruel taunt in those pre-feminist days. She was the one who never challenged her parents, while my father was the one interested in the arts, the one who loved to argue and who challenged them a great deal.

The story about my father that I heard most often when we visited my grandparents in Oakville was the one about him setting fire to Barbara's tricycle. He maintains that this act had more to do with curiosity than anything else, as if he had simply been conducting a scientific experiment. "I wanted to watch it burn," he told me. When I asked him if he'd been happy growing up in Oakville, he said only, "I survived childhood."

I don't think my father ever got the approval from his parents that he wanted. Years later, when he had his own thriving bookstore in Victoria, he still wanted that recognition, but his father never really acknowledged his success as a businessman. His mother was much the same way – withholding praise, refusing to acknowledge his accomplishments – at least until she was much older, after her husband had died, when she was very happy to visit him and his second wife Carole in Victoria, and to have a chance to see her grandchildren.

From a very early age my father found a refuge in art. "I lived in a self-contained world. I had my own little world of my drawing." Every day he drew pictures, most often of ships and trains, a favourite subject being the sinking of the *Titanic*. I have one of his paintings hanging in my living room, a view of a walled town of red brick with snow falling and bare trees in the foreground, one of several he painted when we lived in West Vancouver, before he had the bookstore. When I asked him if I could have this painting, he was overcome by such an attack of modesty that he wouldn't sign it before giving it to me.

My father had his world of drawing, but this is not to say he was shy or introverted; on the contrary, he was bold and enterprising, the instigator of games and activities, getting his friends together to build a flotilla of rafts and to stage mock battles on Lake Ontario, and he was unstoppable when it came to doing the things he wanted to do. When he was seven or eight and wanted to build a boat, he walked to the lumberyard by himself, bought the wood, brought it back on his wagon, and went ahead and nailed it together without help.

As he got older, my father carved out an identity defiantly set apart from his parents', persistently questioning their conventional middle-class values. They were both sporty, but my father had absolutely no interest in sports, no desire to curl and play golf as they did. While they did not like whatever was flamboyant or intellectual or "arty," what sustained him was his love of the arts: drawing, architecture, literature, classical music, interests which he pursued on his own, and drama, which he pursued in high school, where he acted in plays and wrote the mock-Shakespearean satire *Thirteenth Night*. At home he began listening to classical music, especially opera, and buying his own records and playing them for others. One friend remembers being beckoned upstairs "almost conspiratorially" to my father's bedroom to hear his latest classical record.

In a way that is very characteristic of him, my father got over the problem of his parents' disapproval by allying himself with his Munro grandparents, who had more to offer him intellectually and culturally than his parents did. His grandfather had come out from the family farm near Inverness, Scotland, and been a Presbyterian minister in Gladstone, Manitoba, before moving to Oakville and finally Toronto. His grandmother was the first woman to graduate with an M.A. in Mathematics from the University of Manitoba. My father visited these grandparents on Saturdays, after attending art classes in Toronto. His grandfather would engage him in long political arguments, recite the poetry of Robbie Burns, and indulge his interest in architecture by taking him to visit churches all around Toronto. "They spoiled me rotten," he told me, not without satisfaction, the implication being that his grandparents were more fully cognizant of his talents and abilities than his parents ever could be. The circumstances of his grandfather's death indicate how proud he must have been of his grandson's accomplishments. One day the old man went out to buy the paper because he had heard Jim's picture was in it. My father was in a high-school play and photographers had come to the school to take a picture of the cast. Despite his eighty-six years, Grandfather Munro was so excited when he left his apartment to see the paper that he started to sprint across Jarvis Street to get to the newsstand, and he was struck and killed by a car. (It's just the kind of thing I can imagine my father doing, so unrestrained is his enthusiasm for the artistic successes of others.)

Given his love of the arts, it seemed inevitable that my father was destined to meet my mother and fall in love with her. I found it surprising, and somehow reassuring, therefore, to learn that he was attracted to her before he ever knew she was a writer. Naturally, once he did become aware of her literary accomplishments, he was exceedingly – even recklessly – proud of her, and never shy about singing her praises, which made him vulnerable, at least in my mother's eyes. Early on in their courtship he brought home one of her stories for his parents to read, under the mistaken impression that they would appreciate her writing as much as he did. My mother tells me that this put her beyond the pale with her future in-laws right away. Besides being poor, she was not a normal person. Writers, especially women writers, were not quite acceptable in their eyes.

It wasn't until many years later that my mother's career as a writer did become acceptable to them, after she won the Governor General's Award for her first collection of stories, *Dance of the Happy Shades*, in 1968. Being the in-laws of a successful writer, a writer who published books and won prizes, now that was something quite different for them, that was very acceptable indeed. My grandfather went to the awards ceremony and came back to Oakville crowing about meeting Prime Minister Trudeau, even though until that point he had always maintained that he hated Trudeau.

CHAPTER 2

North Vancouver
1952 –1956

BECOMING A MOTHER

When they first moved to Vancouver, my parents rented an apartment in a house on Arbutus Street, across from Kitsilano Beach. My mother got a job at the Kerrisdale library, where she worked part-time for about six months while my father worked at Eaton's, downtown. She draws on this period of her life in the story "Cortes Island" (*The Love of a Good Woman*), in which the young bride, hectored about her marital duties by an older woman, is alarmed by "the peculiar threat" of the china cabinet where all of the knick-knacks had to be washed once a month. Not long afterwards, in 1952, they bought a small house on Kings Road West off upper Lonsdale, high up on the slopes of North Vancouver, a purchase made possible with the gift of a down payment from Arthur Munro.

In my father's photographs, the house looks dark and shadowy, and so it remains in my imagination, a place I lived in before memory, with long ragged grass growing all around, a dim interior (my father did not have a flash), a cat silhouetted in the window, the newly acquired chintz-covered sofa and chair, and my mother, pregnant, illuminated in a patch of sunlight by the fireplace.

That year Arthur Munro came out on a business trip to survey the far-flung Eaton's empire. There are photographs of a visit to the Capilano Suspension Bridge in which he's peering over at the canyon while my mother grips the rail, others of him posing with a fishing rod in hand, the smiling face a softer version of the chiselled, Scottish features of the grandfather I remember. Later my parents take the train up to Lillooet, and my father takes pictures of my mother looking out the train window, her pregnancy fairly advanced by now, a scarf tied over her long hair. In September they are back in North Vancouver; someone has snapped a picture of my mother, my father, and a young boy, a neighbour, sitting on a blanket on the lawn holding kittens, my mother's sailor maternity top ballooning out around her. They look impossibly young.

My mother, shortly before my birth, with my father and a neighbour.

On the next page is a rash of photographs of the new baby girl, Sheila Margaret, wrapped in a blanket, being held by my father, his mother, Margaret Munro, who has come out after the birth, and my mother, who is smiling down at me with her hair falling over her pale face. In another photo my mother and

My father holding me as my mother looks on, in October 1953.

grandmother are sitting side-by-side on a bench outside, preparing the dressing for the Thanksgiving turkey. I notice that even though it's only a week after my birth, my mother has managed to get herself back into her pre-pregnancy slacks. My grandmother is wearing strappy heels and a suit, soft white curls framing a pretty face. The scene looks to be a tableau of domestic harmony, the two women smiling down at the bowl in my grandmother's lap. No one could have guessed at the strain those visits posed for my mother.

It is winter and my grandmother has gone back to Ontario. My mother stands in a clingy knitted dress, ready to push the baby carriage, and I can see patches of melting snow behind her on the road. A little later – it must be early spring since the leaves are still not out – she poses in the backyard in a strapless dress with a fitted bodice and a full skirt made of layers and layers of white net shot through with sequins. (I remember the scratchy feel of that dress when it made its way into the dress-up box years later.) She looks older and more sophisticated partly because her hair is shorter now, cut as a concession to her in-laws, who regarded her long hair as an indication of her unconventional nature. "Why don't you get a haircut?" my grandfather would ask. My father was angry when she cut it. He loved her long hair.

My mother was happy to have given birth to a daughter, relieved and proud to have passed such a major hurdle in the

My mother and my grandmother Munro, preparing the Thanksgiving dinner, 1953.

My mother in the spring of 1954.

female life. When I think of my own birth, I think of the scene in "Mischief" (*Who Do You Think You Are?*), when Rose is in the maternity ward after delivering her baby. "She is still dazed from the birth. Whenever she closed her eyes she saw an eclipse, a big black ball with a ring of fire. That was the baby's head, ringed with pain, the instant before she pushed it out." The actual circumstances of my birth were, in fact, somewhat different. During labour my mother was given something called tincture of opium, and she recalls looking out the window at a brick chimney and the deep blue sky beyond and thinking how beautiful it was. She doesn't remember the experience of giving birth itself, but only of being shut in a room like a broom closet beforehand and wondering if anyone would hear her if she screamed. As was customary at that time, she was kept in the hospital for eight or nine days. The nurses wrapped bindings of heavy cloth around her breasts and middle, for what purpose I do not know. (By the time she went into hospital to have her second baby, tincture of opium was no longer being used. When she asked for it during labour she was told, "Oh we can't use that, it's illegal," and by that time the binding procedure was no longer being followed, either.) Of course my father was not present at my birth. He was out in the waiting room. But from the moment he set eyes on me he adored me. He claimed the day of my birth was the happiest day of his life.

A SLUDGE OF ANIMAL FUNCTION

When she nurses her baby [Kath] often reads a book, sometimes smokes a cigarette, so as not to sink into a sludge of animal function. And she's nursing so that she can shrink her uterus, not just provide the baby – Noelle – with precious maternal antibodies.

– "Jakarta," The Love of a Good Woman

Like Kath in "Jakarta," (whom she saw as a shallow projection of herself), my mother wanted to keep herself from sinking into "a sludge of animal function," to preserve her mind and intellect from the milky, sleepy-eyed torpor that so many other mothers succumbed to. She never smoked when she was nursing me, but she read a lot, and one of the books she was reading was Simone de Beauvoir's feminist manifesto, *The Second Sex*. I wonder what she must have felt reading that book with an infant in her arms. Would she have thought about it when she was rinsing out the diapers, or hanging the tiny clothes out on the line, or pushing me in the stroller? What would she have made of the idea that women have never been fully autonomous beings, that they have always been the Other, defined only in relation to men? Wouldn't she have felt enraged the way I did when I read the book as a teenager?

But when I asked her about it she said no, she did not feel really angry; she thought the book did not describe her own situation. She did tell one journalist in the early seventies, a time when interviews could easily turn into impromptu discussions on feminism, that the book had made her depressed, but that she covered over those feelings. She imagined that de Beauvoir's perceptions applied to women in Europe, but that North American women were more advanced, and not at all oppressed. Besides, her chosen field was so far out of the main-stream (the idea of a Canadian writer of either sex in those days was practically an oxymoron) that conventional mores simply did not apply, and she was lucky enough to have a husband who supported her work. She did not feel that she personally experienced much obvious discrimination; nor did she think it unfair that she had to leave her job at the library as soon as her pregnancy became visible. People still thought pregnancy was a slightly shameful condition then; it was accepted that the thrust of a pregnant belly would upset the patrons; it would be unseemly. The absence of women in posi-tions of power and authority, of women whose opinions were taken seriously, of women politicians, of women journalists outside of the women's pages, of women writers (except maybe for Jane Austen or George Eliot) from university English courses was not an issue, not yet.

My mother's poor background shielded her from the cult of femininity that was so ingrained in middle-class popular culture. She was not encouraged to collect items for a trousseau as Naomi does in *Lives*, though perhaps once she "had her diamond" she did flash it around a little. She did not belong to a sorority at university and there were no wedding showers when she got married. She never bought into the popularization of Freudian ideas about women being naturally submissive, dependent beings who must sublimate their own ambitions into those of husband and children, partly because her values came from an older, predominantly Scottish tradition of faith in a meritocracy, the idea that you could rise up from poverty through hard work and education. It never occurred to her not to excel, even though she was a woman. Contemporary mores about women did not affect her on an intellectual level perhaps because she never encountered them at Western. Ironically, it was those women who were most educated, friends of hers who had gone to better universities than Western, who were more likely to take these ideas seriously, who might actually have read Freud. It was often those women who were least suited for it who tried hardest to deny their intellectual capacities and to conform to the self-abdicating feminine ideal.

THE MONICAS

In those early years in North Vancouver, keeping house and looking after a baby did not seriously interfere with my mother's writing. Housework was nothing new; from the age of twelve she had been doing all the work at home because her mother had Parkinson's disease. She had been composing poems and stories while she made the beds, or washed the dishes, or hung up the laundry. I think housework and writing have always coexisted for her in a kind of uneasy alliance, the one balancing the other, the predictable routines of household tasks giving her a respite from the immensity of the real work, allowing for a shallower, more ordinary state of mind. The room in which she wrote *Lives of Girls and Women* was a laundry room, and her typewriter was surrounded by a washer, a dryer, and an ironing board. In fact, she could write almost anywhere in the house. I might find her reclining on the couch writing in one of her spiral notebooks when I came home from school, or scribbling away at the kitchen table when I came downstairs for breakfast. She'd always put the notebook away without skipping a beat, in the same way that Jane Austen put her embroidery frame over her writing whenever someone came into the room. You'd think she wasn't doing anything more important than making up a grocery list.

After my father went off to work she mopped the floors and shook out the rugs and rinsed out the diapers. She washed and rinsed the clothes and put them through the wringer and hung them out on the clothesline (or put them on wooden racks around the house when it was raining, which it usually was in North Vancouver) and there would still be time for writing. She typed away while I busied myself exploring the yard, tearing the pages out of magazines in the living room, or rolling potatoes across the kitchen floor. And every afternoon after lunch I had a nap. She made sure of that.

No, the most serious threat to her writing didn't come from being a housewife and mother, it came from the neighbourhood women who were always dropping by for coffee unannounced or congregating in her backyard without invitation or dispensing unsolicited advice about housekeeping, like the woman in "Mischief" (*Who?*) who delivers an interminable monologue about how her kitchen cupboards are organized. Years later she spoke to Barbara Frum in an interview for *Maclean's* ("Great Dames," April 1973) about how she hated those morning coffee klatches she was subjected to in North Vancouver. "There used to be these dreadful long domestic conversations about how do you get the diapers whiter or softer, or whatever you're supposed to do with diapers, and I used to think that everybody else really enjoyed them." Those women were like "the Monicas" in "Jakarta" (*Love*), the young mothers Kath and Sonje hear at the beach:

"You can get ground round as cheap as hamburger if you go to Woodward's."
"I tried zinc ointment but it didn't work."
"Now he's got an abscess in the groin."
"You can't use baking powder, you have to use soda."

Kath finds something menacing about their total and unselfconscious capitulation to fifties domesticity, something so powerful it seems to obliterate the natural surroundings.

"They are either frankly pregnant or look as though they might be pregnant, because they have lost their figures . . . hollering out the names of their children. . . . Their burdens, their strung-out progeny and maternal poundage, their authority, can annihilate the bright water, the perfect small cove with the red-limbed arbutus trees, the cedars, growing crookedly out of the high rocks."

That was one kind of woman. Another kind of woman made no attempt to conform to the status quo, like Jocelyn in "Mischief" – with her long braids, her sloppy moccasins, and her copy of André Gide – in the maternity ward with Rose.

Suspecting she has found an ally in Jocelyn, Rose strikes up a
conversation with her after both of them have been subjected
to the description of the kitchen cupboards:

> "I hope you polish your stove knobs," she said quietly.
> "I certainly do," said Jocelyn.
> "Do you polish them every day?"
> "I used to polish them twice a day but now that I have the
> new baby I just don't know if I'll get around to it."
> "Do you use that special stove-knob polish?"
> "I certainly do. And I use the special stove-knob cloths
> that come in that special package."
> "That's good. Some people don't. "
> "Some people will use anything."
> "Old dishrags."
> "Old snotrags."
> "Old snot."

In one interview she has referred to these North Vancouver
neighbours as her "jailers"; unbeknownst to themselves, they
were the major reason my parents moved to West Vancouver
after only three years in that house. West Vancouver was more
affluent than North Vancouver; the yards were bigger, the fences
were higher, and there was more respect for privacy. This was an
important feature, since my mother was not the kind of person
who could say "Sorry, I'm busy," when the neighbours showed
up on her doorstep, who could never tell them, "Look, I'm
writing. Could you come back later?" It was something that my
father could never understand, that really exasperated him.
"Why can't you say you're busy?" he'd implore. "Say you have
an appointment." But for her, such an act of self-assertion

would have been inconceivable, it would be breaking some Laidlaw taboo, upsetting some delicate balance that allowed her to live in two worlds, the world of her surface life and the world of her writing.

My father, me, and my mother, on a trip to Wingham, in 1954.

SUBURBIA

I remember driving with my parents through a new housing subdivision, rows of raw-looking two-storey homes on bare ground, when I was seven or eight years old. I thought about the look of those houses and I said they looked flimsy. My mother praised me for choosing that word. "Yes, that is exactly right, they do look flimsy." (She has written about my penchant for searching out the right word in "Miles City, Montana." Six-year-old Cynthia tries out new words like "image" in the back seat of the car when her family is driving across the continent.) As my use of the word "flimsy" suggests, I picked up the same distrust for the housing divisions that she had, and for what they represented: the suburban dream of the 1950s.

I did not consider our street in West Vancouver as part of suburbia. The homes in our neighbourhood looked old and established; the gardens were landscaped, there were hedges and trees through which you could catch glimpses of gables, windows with leaded panes. I considered Lynn Valley in North Vancouver, where our parents' friends the Browns lived, to be the true suburbia, with its rows of "new, white and shining houses, set side by side in long rows in the wound of the earth" ("The Shining Houses," *Dance of the Happy Shades*). And it wasn't just the outside of the houses. It was what went on inside. At the Browns' we were allowed to drink Coke and eat potato chips and watch *The Beverly Hillbillies* and *Gunsmoke* on TV while the adults talked upstairs. This would have been unheard-of in our household. Once, Mr. Brown took my parents outside to see his new car with the bucket seats, and I realized that was part of suburbia, too. He was showing off, oblivious to my parents' unspoken disapproval, and I felt strangely sorry for him.

My mother has written very little about the years she spent living in Vancouver. "I hated it so much I've never been able to do much with it fictionally," she told one interviewer. One early story that does make use of the Vancouver material is "The Shining Houses," written while she was still living in North Vancouver, in which the shining houses of new suburbia are aggressively displacing "the old wilderness city that had lain on the side of the mountain." A group of neighbours in one of the new subdivisions signs a petition to get rid of a ramshackle property belonging to an older woman who lives down the street. Her sheds and chicken coop are an affront to the new order of conformity and to the respectability of the new houses. The narrator distrusts the new generation and their new order. She won't sign the petition, but she feels powerless against them.

"The Shining Houses" was one of her earliest stories, a fictional retelling of an incident that very much upset her. There was an older woman in the neighbourhood who used to babysit me occasionally, who lived in one of the original North Vancouver properties on which there were shacks and an old apple orchard, a woodpile, maybe a fridge on the front porch. In my mother's words, "really it was quite tidy, but by suburban standards it was a mess." (Of course, by Lowertown standards such a house would be perfectly respectable.) One of the neighbours discovered the house was on a road allowance and he got a petition together to get rid of it, and succeeded. She was the only one who wouldn't sign. "Nobody was on my side, not your dad, believe me. I just felt awful. I was so alone."

WRITING

Through these early years my mother was always writing or trying to write, dashing back to the typewriter after the grandparents had gone, when I was having a nap, when the neighbours finally decamped. She was getting stories published in magazines. The first of these, "A Basket of Strawberries," came out in the November 1953 edition of the Canadian magazine *Mayfair* (it folded soon afterwards) a month after my birth. My mother was twenty-two years old. "The Idyllic Summer" and

"At the Other Place" came out in *The Canadian Forum* in 1954 and 1955, respectively; "The Edge of Town" appeared in *Queen's Quarterly* in 1955, and three stories were accepted by *Chatelaine* magazine in 1956. In those days there was far more demand than now for fiction in magazines, and the pay was surprisingly good. "A Basket of Strawberries" netted three hundred dollars, and the *Chatelaine* stories earned her three hundred and fifty dollars apiece. The money counted for a significant part of the family income, and it was partly on the strength of these sales that my parents decided to go ahead with the purchase of the house in West Vancouver. (Though not yet the preserve of the rich and famous it subsequently became – except for the exclusive British Properties up on the slopes of Grouse Mountain – West Vancouver was just barely within their financial reach.) There were rejections as well, rejections from *The New Yorker*, where she was already sending her work, manuscripts that had to be abandoned, and attempts at writing novels that didn't go anywhere, but overall she was fairly successful in those early years, quite prolific, really, considering her situation as a wife and young mother who underwent three pregnancies between the ages of twenty-one and twenty-six. Stories later collected in *Dance of the Happy Shades* were written at this time as well. "Thanks for the Ride" (first published in *The Tamarack Review*, Winter 1957) was written when I was about six months old. My mother remembers seeing me smiling at her from my crib when she was writing it. It was the first time I had smiled at her first, and she took it as a good omen. "Day of the Butterfly," originally published as "Good-By Myra" (*Chatelaine* magazine, July 1956) and "The Time of Death" (*The Canadian Forum*, June 1956) and "The Shining Houses" (*Anthology*) also date from the North Vancouver period.

During these years she was submitting many of her stories to the editor and broadcaster Robert Weaver for his CBC Radio series *Canadian Short Stories* (later *Anthology*). He became a literary lifeline for her, as he was for so many other emerging Canadian writers, particularly short-story writers (a role that was recognized when he was awarded the Order of Canada in the year 2000). She had actually begun sending him stories when she was still at university; in May of 1951 she had submitted "The Strangers" and "The Widower" (one of the stories published in *Folio*). He accepted "The Strangers" but had this to say of "The Widower": "you have failed to rise above somewhat commonplace and tedious material." It was always hit-and-miss with the CBC submissions; "The Man Who Goes Home" and "The Liberation" were approved, but "The Shivaree" and "The Man from Melbury" were both rejected, and the editors were unanimous in their distaste for "Thanks for the Ride," the much anthologized story later published in *Dance of the Happy Shades*, which editor Joyce Marshall found "a bit 'dubious' and very outspoken." They were worried about the language (there was a CBC policy against broadcasting four-letter words) and Weaver reported to a colleague that it was "the one which all of us liked least." (When my father read this story he was convinced it was one of her best, as good a story as anyone anywhere had ever written.)

In his letters, Robert Weaver was not afraid to be critical, tempering his criticism with praise, to be sure, but in his quintessentially Canadian way, never becoming effusive, never gushing. He did not say a story was "great" or he "loved it"; he never used the superlatives that later came to be associated with her work. He said things like "you present your material with real integrity" or "you are one of the very few really interesting writers to appear in Canada over the past half-dozen years." Guessing shrewdly, he told a colleague that Alice was "the kind of writer who won't fold up under firm criticism and I don't think we need to take stories from her simply because we are afraid she might otherwise stop writing altogether."

Besides critiquing the stories, Weaver was helpful to her in recommending magazines she might submit to, names of editors she might contact, in Canada and in the United States and Britain, and he kept her apprised of news on the literary scene. After 1957, he solicited her stories for his fledgling literary magazine, *The Tamarack Review*. (He thought it especially fitting that "Mrs. Cross and Mrs. Kidd" [*The Moons of Jupiter*] was published in the very last issue of that magazine in 1982, because one of her stories had been published in its second issue, twenty-five years before.)

He came to visit her once, in North Vancouver. He described being greeted at the door by a "smashingly beautiful" woman with a baby in her arms. She invited him in and since she didn't have any alcohol in the house, and believed that people in literary circles had to be offered a drink, she didn't offer him anything at all. Finally, in a parched voice, he asked for a drink of water.

READING

My mother has told me that until she was twenty-three or so her writing was consciously imitative. She wanted to write like Virginia Woolf or Henry James, exploring the minute problems in people's lives, trying to get at some ineffable experience. She wanted to capture some atmosphere about a place, some feeling that was important, to get at "the exact texture of how things are." In her own estimation, the stories she was writing were so loaded down with description that she hardly had time to get around to the characters and what happened to them.

Surprisingly for someone who later would say that all her writing was "in essence autobiographical," at this time she was not introspective. She was not very interested in herself or in using material from her own life. Writing was not a form of self-expression or therapy. Nor was it a matter of social conscience, or a need to explore issues and ideas. She told me her subject was then, and remains to this day, "human life." She can't understand how writers choose a theme and then write about *that*, or consciously choose symbols. Her desire is to enter into the experience of other people, to gain access to realities other than her own, to pull away a curtain and reveal "some dazzling mystery." The critic and writer Kent Thompson put his finger on her particular genius during a CBC Radio panel discussion when he said, "She imagines reality accurately."

In those North Vancouver years she immersed herself in the "Southern Gothic" writers: Carson McCullers, Flannery O'Connor, and the one she most admired, Eudora Welty, whose fictional worlds of poverty, intolerance, and eccentricity in small Southern towns resonated so much with her own experience growing up in Huron County. James Agee's novel *A Death in the Family*, and his account of poor sharecroppers in the Southern states, *Let Us Now Praise Famous Men*, had a tremendous impact on her as well. What she loved about these writers was the way they created a world you could see and experience, "something as simple as the description of a street and you could see yourself walking down that street, you knew just exactly how it was." A novel she read at this time was *Independent People* by Halldor Laxness, winner of the Nobel

Prize in 1955 and only recently back in print. The book had a magical quality she was trying to capture in her own work, and while it hinted at the supernatural, it was not at all romantic, and was set in that bleakest of environments, an Icelandic farm. My mother still vividly remembers a scene in which the pregnant farmer's wife butchers a sheep; another description she loved has the young boy waking up in the farmhouse and imagining that all the pots and pans hanging on the wall are animate. Chekhov was another writer she greatly admired, especially his ability to create a world that could be fully felt, fully experienced. And all through these early years she was reading *The New Yorker* religiously, along with the short-story anthologies *Discovery* and *New World Writing*, and discovering contemporary writers like Edna O'Brien, John Cheever, Saul Bellow, and J.D. Salinger, along with more established authors like Katherine Anne Porter and Elizabeth Bowen.

MOTHERHOOD

"I'm just so terribly glad that I had my children when I did. I'm terribly grateful that I had them. Yet, I have to realize, I probably wouldn't have had them if I had the choice."
– from an interview in *The London Free Press*, June 22, 1974

By the time she was twenty-five years old, an age when I was not even contemplating marriage, let alone having children, my mother had already been through three pregnancies. Birth control in this era before the Pill allowed women to limit the size of their families, but wasn't usually reliable enough to prevent pregnancy altogether. What I find remarkable is the amount of work she was able to get done during that time, despite the morning sickness, the fatigue and lassitude that tend to take over, the breastfeeding, the endless diaper changing, the sleepless nights. How did she do it? I know when I was pregnant and the mother of an infant, the thought of any creative or intellectual endeavour beyond reading a newspaper (and even then I never read an article from beginning to end) was something very far from my mind. I remember having to finish one of the last book reviews I had agreed to do, sitting at my word processor while my four-month-old son James lay wailing on the bed behind me. I had to keep typing and typing, feeling wretched and exhausted, all through his cries so I could meet my deadline.

She kept working, but as time went on my mother found the balancing act of writing and mothering more difficult. When I got to be a little older, after the euphoria of having produced a baby had worn off, my mother began to have second thoughts about how she would manage. She had to write – not only to write, but to write a masterpiece – and how could she possibly write a masterpiece with me dragging her fingers off the typewriter keys or pulling the pencil out of her hand. "Come and see," I would command, "come and see," and she would fend me off with one hand while keeping her other hand on the typewriter keys, the fragile thread of her narrative slipping from her grasp.

How well I know this feeling, this sense of having to be on the surface of life, not really thinking, not focussing, sitting on the edge of the sandbox while my three-year-old plays, following him around and around the garden, all those hours with trains and trucks and stories, wondering what to have for dinner, when all the time you want to go deeper, when all the time you are desperate to get to some other part of yourself.

"Come and see." My mother and me at the North Vancouver house in 1954 or '55.

The stories my mother told about me. It is lunch time. My mother puts a cup of milk in front of me in my high-chair and I fling it in her face. She lifts me out of the high-chair, carries me into the bedroom, and throws me onto the bed so hard that I bounce onto the floor. (She now says I didn't really bounce onto the floor but that is how I remember the story being told.) This incident takes place after she has brought me downtown on three different buses and we've had to wait in line at Eaton's so I could have my picture taken. I was tired and cranky by then and she wouldn't buy me the toy that I wanted.

We're about to go for a walk. I run outside and bring the stroller around to the sidewalk and seat myself in it. But I'm too big for the stroller. I'm old enough to walk. A little older, I do agree to walk, but I won't hold her hand crossing the street. I go limp and lie down on the road and have to be dragged across.

The point about these stories, at least the way I have interpreted them, is that they are about my particular character, rather than just being a rueful description of the exasperating way two-year-olds normally behave. The picture I have is of a mother who should still have been at university, the way I was at that age, who was impatient, withholding, "emotionally tight" as she put it, towards her strong-willed and demanding toddler, not only because her writing was of such overwhelming importance to her, which it was, but more because of her youth and inexperience. I see her like the young mother in "Tell Me Yes or No" in the 1974 collection *Something I've Been Meaning to Tell You*, weighed down by adult responsibilities and domestic drudgery. "I was sleepily rinsing diapers, clad in a red corduroy dressing gown, wet across the stomach; I was pushing a baby carriage or a stroller along the side of the road to the store . . ." I see my mother and me engaged in a power struggle, a struggle which I lost eventually, capitulating after many battles, emerging from the crucible of those first years compliant, eager to please, GOOD.

THE BABY THAT DIED

One of the reasons my mother found me so trying was that before I was even a year old, she found herself pregnant again. It was not a planned pregnancy and she did not know how she would be able to write with a toddler and a tiny baby to look after. This was the baby my mother lost, the baby named Catherine, *the baby that died*. My sister Jenny and I knew that she had red hair because our father saw her. We knew he thought she was a Mongoloid baby because of the way she looked, but really she looked this way because she didn't have any kidneys. We knew that she lived for fourteen hours. My father claims he doesn't remember any of this.

In the early hours after the birth, before the extent of the problems were known, my mother and father talked about getting the baby into an institution of some kind. For my mother, the prospect of having to care for a child with Down's syndrome after looking after her mother for all those years would have meant the death of her creative self. This was a sacrifice she was not willing to make at a time in her life when she was just beginning to realize her potential as a writer. Of course, this proved to be unnecessary.

Years later she had a tombstone erected for Catherine in a cemetery in North Vancouver's Lynn Valley; she could no longer bear the thought of the baby being buried in an unmarked grave. She visits it once a year if she can, bringing flowers. To me, this business of arranging for a gravesite was a surprising thing for my mother to do. I don't associate symbolic gestures and ritual observances of this sort with her. It was all the more unexpected because in the years when Jenny and I were growing up, the death of our sister was not considered anything especially sad or tragic. It was just something that happened in our family, part of the family history.

There are no photographs of my mother when she was pregnant with Catherine, and the death was something she rarely mentioned. It wasn't until I had children myself that I came to understand how she would have been affected by it. For years afterwards she had dreams about a lost baby, dreams about leaving a baby girl out in the rain and forgetting about her, a theme that crops up in the recent story "My Mother's Dream" (*The Love of a Good Woman*). The dream kept recurring until my sister Jenny was born after we had moved to West Vancouver.

Now I can understand why she was so protective, why she followed Jenny to school, hiding behind cars in case Jenny turned around and saw her, and why she wouldn't let Jenny out of the yard even though I had been allowed to roam the neighbourhood and go down to the creek by the time I was four or five. A friend wrote to her soon after Jenny's birth, "I'm glad to hear your maternal instinct has made its appearance. From what I've heard the first one usually does get the short end in that respect." Even today, as I am "the first one," these words give me pause. "Appearance," not reappearance. My mother told me, "Jenny was a gift. I didn't have nearly the expectations of Jenny that I had of you." I felt that keenly as I was growing up. Jenny was fussed over and babied far more than I was. I felt loved, but that the love I received was more the result of being earned, whereas Jenny came by love naturally, just for being herself.

CHAPTER 3

West Vancouver
1956 –1959

THE HOUSE IN WEST VANCOUVER

I walk up the path, and open the heavy wooden gate flanked by the tall laurel hedge. It is a sunny morning in May. I've just come back from Sunday School at the Unitarian Church and I'm wearing a white hat with a spray of artificial flowers and pearls attached to it, and lacy white gloves. Closing the gate behind me, I stand there leaning against it, looking up the tiers of steps leading to the front door, at the mountain ash tree with its white confetti blossoms drifting down onto the lawn and the rock garden, the huge chestnut tree to my left and the playhouse my father built, where I staged puppet shows for the neighbours.

I love all the places in our yard. I love the mountain ash tree I can climb, with its bright orange berries in the fall, the yellow roses blooming against the high wooden fence, the miniature Japanese maple tree that spreads a maroon canopy over my head, the grape arbour by the kitchen with its tender yellow-green leaves, its delicate and bitter fruit, and the sloping lawn

Me in the front yard of the house in West Vancouver, in 1955 or '56.

for practising handstands and cartwheels on and rolling down until I feel sick and my head is spinning.

The house sits on a terrace above the rock garden. The kitchen, dining room, and living room face the front, looking south, and through the large picture windows it is possible to catch a glimpse of the ocean. There are two bedrooms at either end of a long, dim hallway at the back.

The dining room is painted French blue and has a crystal chandelier over the table. I see my mother standing on the table polishing each crystal drop with a mixture of baking soda and water, the sparkling drops reflecting tints of blue and lilac. In the sideboard there are sterling-silver dishes and serving spoons (my mother always used one of these spoons for digging in the garden; it wouldn't have occurred to her to buy a trowel). It is my job to polish them on Saturdays and I rub the dull, tarnished silver with a rag soaked in silver polish until I can see my own face reflected on the trays and the gravy boat, and the oval dishes with their fitted lids. The silver came from Grandmom and Granddad, who lived "back east."

Down in the basement there is an old wringer washer. I see my mother feeding the sheets and pillowcases and diapers and dresses through the moving rollers so they come out, flat as pancakes, into the washbasin on the other side, then hanging them up to dry on wooden racks. We are never, never to get anywhere near those rollers in case our hand or arm gets caught. When the clothes are dry, she takes them upstairs and I hear the thump and hiss of the iron as she presses out all the creases in the frills and sashes and puffed sleeves of the dresses I wore.

In the living room my sister Jenny and I sit on the floor in front of our new television. We watch the Lone Ranger's horse rear up to the music of the *William Tell* Overture, the Lone Ranger with his sensitive mouth, black mask, low-slung holster, and white tights. On the black-and-white screen we watch *The Three Stooges* and Popeye cartoons, Olive Oyl crooning "OOHH POPeye" and twirling her legs together, that ultimate symbol of female fecklessness and imbecility. Behind us, our mother sits in the armchair in a gloomy corner, sipping a cup of coffee in a ruminating, reflective way.

Tucked away in the darkest corner of my parents' dark bedroom is a small table with a typewriter on it. That is where my mother writes. I don't remember dragging her fingers off the keys, but I do recall fooling around with it once and jamming

*Jenny and me watching television, as my mother
reads in the background, 1961.*

some of the keys. I gathered that this was a serious transgression
and I did not touch the typewriter again.

In the mornings my father takes the bus from 27th and
Marine Avenue across the Lions Gate Bridge and through
Stanley Park to his job downtown in the fabric department of
Eaton's department store. We have a car, a Morris Oxford,
which my father is quite proud of, but he takes the bus because
it's easier and because Lions Gate is a toll bridge at this time.
My sister Jenny and I like to hide in the recesses of the laurel
hedge at the corner of the street when he comes home from
work. We jump out and yell "Surprise!" when he reaches us
after walking up the hill from the bus stop, and we run to his
open arms. Sometimes he brings me beautiful scraps of brocade

fabric samples, metallic threads of silver and gold fashioned into leaves and flowers, which I treasure and make into dresses for my dolls. Like me, my father loves the house and the yard in West Vancouver, and we are both nostalgic about that period in our family history. It was our family before the fall, before the glares, the slamming doors, the mutual contempt that flourished between us like some poisonous weed when I became an adolescent.

I see him outside in the sunshine smoothing and patting a new patch of cement where he is redoing the front walk. He is smiling and from time to time he starts humming to himself, something by Handel, the *Music for the Royal Fireworks*, perhaps, or "See the Conquering Hero Come." Sometimes he even chuckles to himself as if there is a running comedy show going on in his head. It doesn't matter what he is doing, whether it's clipping the hedge, or mowing the grass, or burning huge piles of leaves in the fall, he tackles everything with the same nervous energy and enjoyment. Yet his mood is not predictable; it can darken suddenly along with a change in the weather. On a cloudy day when it looks like rain he peers anxiously up at the sky, scanning the clouds for a patch of blue. "Oh, no," he says, as if the weather is deliberately, maliciously trying to ruin his happiness. It was always the same with accidents. If you broke a plate or a glass it was a catastrophe. He would tell you, "Oh nooo . . . look what you've done," as if you didn't know, and then he would glare at you as you swept up the pieces.

The house in West Vancouver bore the stamp of my father's personality, his tastes, his interests in art and music. In our basement he improvised, painting a huge black circle on the cement floor with a pattern of orange and black triangles inside it, like a circular Mondrian. Upstairs were paintings he'd done, and his records lined the shelves in the living room: boxed sets of *Don Giovanni* (my mother's favourite music in the world), *The Magic Flute* with Papageno decked in feathers on the cover, *Faust*, *The Messiah*, *Carmen*, *La Traviata*, *The Barber of Seville*. At the far end of the room there was an old pump organ with the *Fireside Book of Folk Songs* open at "Drink to Me Only with Thine Eyes." I tried to learn the organ by myself, plunking out "Good King Wenceslas" with one finger, but I never took lessons and that was about as far as I got. On top of the organ, along with two recorders, was my father's French horn, acquired when he traded in the trumpet he used to play in the basement. The more muted tones of the French horn were perhaps a concession to the neighbours. Sometimes he puts on a record, takes the instrument from its place, and stands with it poised in the air waiting for the horn section to begin. Then he plays along with the music, his cheeks bulging and ruddy, his eyes tearing from exertion and excitement.

My mother was different. I see her digging in the dirt with a large silver spoon in a desultory way, or checking to see if the nasturtiums she planted are coming up. She did not assert herself in the house the way my father did. The chintz furniture, the classical records, the chandelier, even the house itself were my father's choices, not hers. She lived there but she did not take possession, not ever. She was like the young mother in "Miles City, Montana," who sees herself as a detached observer. "In my own house, I seemed to be often looking for a place to hide . . . so that I could get busy at my real work, which was a sort of wooing of distant parts of myself. I lived in a state of siege, always losing just what I wanted to hold on to. But on trips there was no difficulty. I could be talking to Andrew, talking to the children and looking at whatever they wanted me to look at . . . and all the time these bits and pieces would be flying together inside me. The essential composition would be achieved. This made me hopeful and lighthearted. It was being a watcher that did it. A watcher, not a keeper." I have often thought of these words in connection with how she appeared as a mother to me when I was growing up.

My mother in 1958 or '59, in Vancouver.

The truth was that, in spite of escaping "the Monicas," she did not like living in the new house, which she didn't think she and my father could afford, or the big yard, or the neighbourhood. After growing up in such poverty, she really didn't feel comfortable with the level of affluence and the unashamed materialism of the fifties that such a house represented. It was what my father wanted, not what she wanted. How could she be living in relative luxury while her father was struggling to make a living as a night watchman at the foundry in Wingham after the failure of his mink and fox farm?

She must have expressed these reservations in a letter to her younger sister Sheila, for I have a letter full of reassurances that Sheila wrote to her soon after the house was purchased. "It doesn't matter whether you live in a new beautiful house or a few little rooms, that doesn't change anything, not you or what we feel towards you, not your own inside feeling and thought and enthusiasm toward life. . . . If you were in dirty little rooms you would not complain or feel they affected your happiness with Jim. And it is the same with luxury in this new house."

My mother did not like the rain and gloom that are an inevitable part of Vancouver's climate. And she always had a strange feeling about the dense bushes and shrubs around the house and the Douglas-fir trees looming behind it, as if the forest were pressing in on her. It was a very unfamiliar kind of landscape, and the edge of the rainforest must have seemed claustrophobic after the wide open spaces of rural Ontario, the brightness of snow-covered fields in winter. The bushes and trees seemed to have some kind of malevolent presence, as if something was lurking in them. For many years after she moved away from West Vancouver she had a recurring dream about being back in that house and having to live those years all over again. The force of the bushes was always in that dream.

"WANT TO LOVE YOU!"

My earliest memory about my mother takes place in the kitchen of the house in West Vancouver and is not a real memory, it's a dream. In the dream, my mother has turned into a witch with a black pointed hat and a black gown, just like a Hallowe'en witch. She puts me into the roasting pan and shoves me in the oven. When she takes me out, I am a roast turkey.

A true memory, not a dream: I am holding up a chair, threatening to attack my mother if she doesn't stop singing in French, but she goes on in that quavery, ingenuous voice of hers, *Frère Jacques, Frère Jacques, dormez-vous, dormez-vous, sonnez les matins, sonnez les matins, ding dong bell.* I brandish the legs of the chair at her like a lion tamer but still she doesn't stop. She is taunting me just for fun. I can tell by the way she keeps smiling.

Another memory: I'm lying in bed and I pull the covers over my head and lie perfectly still. My mother is coming. She comes into the bedroom and lies down on top of me. "This is a nice comfortable rock to lie on," she says. "I think I'll just go to sleep." I start to wiggle and squirm. "Hey, what is happening? This rock is moving." I squirm some more and she pulls the cover off my head. "Hey, this isn't a rock at all. It's my little girl."

My mother recites rhymes to me. One goes:

There was a little girl
Who had a little curl
Right in the middle of her forehead
When she was good, she was very, very good
And when she was bad, she was HORRID.

Another was one she made up:

Little Miss Munro
Where do you go?
Bright and early in the morning

I'm going downtown
To buy a golden crown
Bright and early in the morning.

Most of the time I was good, but then there were the times when she got the wooden spoon out of the kitchen drawer and spanked me, whack, whack, whack, on my bare bottom. She has since told me that I would cry out "Want to love you, want to love you!" when the punishment was about to be administered. Afterwards I would lie in tears on the bed, feeling utterly dejected, thinking my mother was never, ever going to come to console me. The last time she spanked me I remember well. She had taken my sister Jenny and me to an exclusive dress shop in the Village, the main shopping district of West Van, and we were roaring around the change rooms while she was trying on clothes until finally Jenny knocked down a glass display case. All the way home on the bus, she did not speak to us. I knew what was coming, but this time I thought of a subterfuge and cried a little harder than I had to when the wooden spoon came down, and, miraculously, the spanking stopped after only two or three whacks. Until then I had not known I could deceive her.

My mother is coming up the walk carrying a bag of groceries. She stops, takes off her Jackie Kennedy sunglasses, tosses her hair, and looks over at me with her smiling red mouth. My mother is younger and prettier than the other mothers. When she comes to my school, people say she could be my sister.

I am standing in the bathroom doorway watching my mother apply lipstick with a kind of expertise you did not usually see with her, colouring the top lip in and smacking her lips together. She has a different expression when she looks in the mirror, one eyebrow arched up a little more than usual as she combs it with a tiny black brush, and her mouth is a little pouty-looking. She is wearing a short-sleeved dress stretched tightly over pointed breasts, cinched in at the waist and flaring out in a full skirt. I comment on how small her waist is. "I have an excellent figure," she says, patting powder onto her face with a pink pad, "but don't tell anyone I told you that." She puts the pad back inside the round black compact and snaps it shut.

My young mother, around age 30, in West Vancouver.

Once, I remember staring at the blue and purple tracings on her ankle that looked like a nest of worms. "You did that to me," she said. "You did that when you were two years old." She meant that I had kicked her there. I looked again at the veins, amazed and ashamed at my ability to cause her permanent injury. They were now part of the road map of her varicose veins, ropy, blue tracks that bulged under the skin; I thought they were "very close" veins, which meant they were very close to the skin. Years later, she would undergo operations to have them stripped, and I would imagine them being ripped out of her legs like tree branches being stripped from a tree.

A SECRET LIFE

Unlike the writer Hugo, the husband in "Material" (*Something I've Been Meaning to Tell You*) who forges an identity out of being a writer, my mother did not become part of any literary community; nor did she go out of her way to befriend individual writers. She admired the work of the celebrated Vancouver writer Ethel Wilson but never met her. She got together with Margaret Laurence, who was living with her husband and young children in the Kitsilano neighbourhood across town. They discussed the feasibility of ironing husbands' shirts, but they never got to know each other well. The only writer friend that I remember visiting was the poet Elizabeth Gourlay. We had lunch with her at her mansion in the exclusive Kerrisdale neighbour-hood. There were beautiful, tall flower borders in the back garden, and lunch, I seem to recall, was formal and elegant. Women writers at that time had to keep their writing an under-cover, clandestine operation and pretend that home and family and housework were the only important things in their lives.

That was one reason for my mother's avoiding other writers. Another had to do with the work she was doing being so important to her, the creative process so fragile and precarious, that she had to protect it at all costs. Drawing attention to herself as a writer was the last thing she wanted to do.

She did not show her stories to anyone before they were published, except my father, who was allowed to read them only when they were finished. Nor did she talk about what she was writing, or say how the work was going. (She asks other writers "How's the writin' goin'?" as a joke.) In her mind, talking about what you were writing was just inviting trouble, and could even sabotage what you were doing. This is a sobering thought, considering all the workshops, the writers' groups, the supportive critiquing, the work-in-progress author readings that go on in the literary scene today, but clearly she was (and is) wise to keep her writing private, since it works for her. She has had bad experiences when she didn't. Once she asked my father to read a story of hers that had been rejected. He said he didn't like the story as much as some of her others, and she proceeded to burn the manuscript. Later the editor wrote to her saying that he did want the story after all, and of course she didn't have a copy and had to write it all over again from scratch.

A REGULAR MOTHER

"Your mother always had a huge guilt feeling about writing because you kids theoretically were being neglected while she was trying to write. She spent a lot of time with you kids, too, but she really wanted to write and she didn't want to be a regular mother."
    – from an unpublished interview with Jim Munro

I am making valentines, cutting out pictures of kittens from a deck of playing cards, pasting each one onto a red heart, then pasting each heart onto a white paper doily. I leave what I am doing and go into the kitchen where my mother is squeezing pink icing from a wax-paper tube into pink hearts on a batch of heart-shaped cookies on a cookie sheet. Her hands are shaking and the pink hearts come out all wobbly. Tactfully, I say nothing and pretend not to notice.

My mother did the things that other mothers did. She baked cookies and blackberry pies (picking blackberries from the bushes beside the back lane was one of our summer rituals), and made ambitious desserts like zabaglione and trifle. Once she even tried Baked Alaska but forgot about it in the oven. She decorated the bedroom I shared with Jenny with blue chenille bedspreads and curtains in a pattern of green and blue birds. She put on elaborate birthday parties for me, as grand as any in the neighbourhood, where we played "London Bridge Is Falling Down" and "Pin the Tail on the Donkey." The year I turned eight, she baked a cake with HAPPY BIRTHDAY written on it in chocolate chips, the occasion marred a little when everyone sang, "Happy Birthday to you/Happy Birthday to you/You look like a monkey/And you act like one too." She brought me ginger ale and vanilla ice cream when I was sick. "Don't take rides from strangers," she reminded me. "Remember to say thank you for the nice time. Be careful crossing the street."

And yet she was not really like other mothers. One of my friends at that time was Gwennie, who had a mother but no father. Gwennie had one fat red ringlet down her back, a pug nose, and a face covered with freckles. She and her mother lived in the upstairs of an old house, in dark rooms with sloping walls. Once when I'd been visiting, I was standing in the kitchen looking up at the ceramic wall plaque of a black woman with bulging cheeks and a basket of fruit on her head, and Gwennie's mother gave me a big hug and a bag of cookies to take home with me. I walked home in a state of elation, going over and over what I would say to my mother about how she could be more like Gwennie's mother. I found her down-stairs sweeping the basement floor and launched into my little speech about how happy my friend's mother had made me. "You could give me hugs like that," I said. She gave me a terrible look, turned away, and kept on sweeping.

The party for my seventh birthday, 1960.

My mother did not like doing anything that required manual dexterity or hand-eye coordination. She did not drive a car. She did not play tennis or badminton. I never saw her throw a ball. She didn't take photographs because her hands would shake and the pictures would be blurred. She did not knit or crochet or do embroidery as her grandmother had, or sew like a friend of hers who was famous for making her own wedding dress, all the bridesmaid's dresses, *and all their gloves*. She always took her sunglasses off before crossing the street, as if she did not quite trust herself in the physical world.

My mother and I are reminiscing about West Vancouver as we're waiting for lunch to arrive at the Old House Restaurant in Courtenay, a place we have chosen for its atmosphere more than its food; it has cosy interconnecting rooms with fireplaces, windows with leaded panes, one huge private booth that came in handy when I was nursing Thomas years ago. I look out the window to the pond with the stone bridge across it and remember the time that my older son James ran outside and waded into the pond when he was a toddler, and also remember the puddle of muddy water under the table that we left behind. We have been coming here for close to ten years. Today we are alone, sipping white wine (we always order white wine), chatting about the move to West Vancouver, and when the food arrives my mother tells me matter-of-factly, almost as an aside, "I didn't have much interaction with you after that." But how was that possible, I was thinking as I bent over my seafood fettucini. I wasn't even three years old at the time that we moved.

I tell myself that's the way it was then. There were clearer boundaries between parents and children, separate pastimes and entertainments. Parents were not always going to watch their kids play hockey or baseball or soccer, or driving their children to school and swimming and skating and music lessons and birthday parties, or volunteering in the classroom. "Go play," my father would say if we were inside the house. Or, after there was television, "Turn that thing off and go outside and play."

Of course there was more to it than that. My mother has spoken of her need to hold back so she could give what she needed to give to her writing. I think I was a threat to her more than either of my sisters ever were, partly because of being the firstborn and partly because of my temperament. She told me once that she did not hold me or touch me much unless she was dressing me or changing me, and she couldn't believe that my father wanted to play with me all day long on his days off. The family life she lived with us was not her real, true life. That was the solitary life she led at her writing desk.

My mother has talked about wanting to be the opposite kind of mother from her own mother, whom she saw as moralistic, demanding, smothering, and emotionally manipulative. I asked her if she had chosen her hands-off approach as a way of protecting us from what she had gone through with her mother.

"I wasn't so much protecting you, let's say, I wasn't thinking of you so much as myself, and the image of myself as a mother, as totally different. I was going to be a mother who didn't enforce a great big generation gap, I was going to be a mother who valued you for your idiosyncrasies, for your real selves as I thought them. Let's say I was thinking of the kind of mother I would be, not what it would do to you."

When I read Louisa May Alcott's *Little Women*, I used to amuse myself by wondering whether I was more like Meg, the pretty, responsible oldest daughter, or Jo, the tomboy who sold her hair to make money for the family, or Amy, who is vain and shallow, the one who wins Laurie's heart when you know he really should have married Jo. The only March sister I did not identify with was saintly, sickly Beth, who knitted mittens and dropped them out her window to the poor children in the snow when she was dying. The mother, Marmee, was saintly and good, too, and in our family we referred to her as Smarmy. We despised the piety and sentimentality surrounding Marmee. Our mother was always Mom, and she was never like that.

In our family we did not go to Church. My parents were set against dogma and ritual, and the whole idea of original sin, but once when I was about five years old some friends took me to Sunday School at their church, a Baptist Church, I believe. In the church basement where the Sunday School was held the words of the 23rd psalm were written on the blackboard. We all recited the verses and when I got to the words, "Lo, though I walk through the valley of the shadow of death" I saw a man walking through the depths of a desert canyon, and when I read "my cup runneth over," I saw a huge chalice with a fountain of water gushing over the rim and splashing down around it.

After one of these Sunday School classes I came home in a state of great excitement. I remember rushing into the kitchen where my mother was making lunch and telling her the story about Adam and Eve and how Jesus had died for our sins. It was surprising to me that here was something my parents didn't know about that I had to explain to them. My mother listened politely but she didn't say anything, and after that I didn't go back to the Baptist Church. Soon we were going to the Unitarian Church, where the concept of sin did not come up, where even the word "God" was hardly mentioned, and where I learned instead about the Brotherhood of Man – and gave all the money I had to a foster family somewhere in South America.

BALLET DANCER

I close the French doors of the living room with ritualistic precision, put the record on the turntable, lower the needle carefully, and take up my position in the middle of the room. I wait for the sound of galloping horses and the distant refrain of the Red Army Chorus, holding myself still until the voices grow louder and I begin to dance, leaping and twirling around the room, allowing the music to tell my body what to do next.

My parents took me to the ballet when I was very little, and after that I knew I had to dance. Soon I was taking ballet lessons down in Dundarave with Joy Camden, who looked like a gypsy with her peasant blouses and flounced skirts. I was three years old. At the end of the lesson she would put on some music and let us improvise, and I would be caught up in that wave of the music bearing me along: this phrase would require an arc of the arms, this one call for a leap, another would twirl me around like a dervish. Technically, I was never very good at ballet. I would curl my toes under in an effort to get my feet to turn outwards at a ninety-degree angle like you were supposed to, and Miss Camden would have to come over and straighten them out. In those early years, though, my imperfections did not matter. I was confident in my status as a ballerina, performing at a garden party in my white tutu, providing entertainment at birthday parties, dancing at a little stone church downtown after having my picture taken for the newspaper, practising arabesques and pliés in the living room while the family looked on. "Nobody claps for drawing," observed my sister Jenny dryly.

My father was the one who took me to my recitals and watched me dance, and I did so happily; the smouldering resentment that had to do with sensing his need for me to perform, his too-intense appreciation, had not yet taken hold. He loved to see me as his pretty ballerina, his dancing doll, like Nora in the Ibsen play *A Doll's House,* and he liked nothing better than to watch me. Even before I took up ballet, when I was two, he used to dress me in a little pink dress and show me off to his friends. My mother did not like it. She did not think it was right.

When my mother wanted to have time for writing (I don't think we were ever told what she was doing, but I knew that she wanted everyone out of the house), he would take me on expeditions; we went rowing on Lost Lagoon, or pony-riding in Stanley Park, or swimming at Ambleside beach. Just down the hill from us the tides of the Pacific swept up Georgia Strait and then into Burrard Inlet and the port of Vancouver. Once, we launched our rowboat, inauspiciously named *Titanic II*, at the stony beach down the hill from our house. We carried the boat over the beach and eased it into the water, my ankles stinging from cuts on the barnacle-encrusted rocks, and took turns rowing all along the shore of West Vancouver as far as the Lions Gate Bridge, my hands blistering from the roughness of the oars, which made me rather proud, pulling closer to the long ships sailing under the bridge. It was at times like these that my father was happiest.

When I was eight or nine he began taking me to the movies, usually the ones my mother did not want to see. Both my parents were enthusiastic movie-goers and my mother had to see every movie Elizabeth Taylor was in (she has always had an intense fascination with the violet-eyed star), but the big epic productions of the early sixties didn't appeal to her. He took me to *Ben Hur*, with its bloody chariot race and its ragged slaves in chains rowing (possibly with blistered hands) in the hold of a warship, and the lepers living in a cave. He took my friend Anne and me to the 1963 movie version of *The Phantom of the Opera*, with the man in the mask taking the opera singer to his cave under the opera house and making her sing the same song over and over again. And he took me to a musical about a stripper named Gypsy Rose Lee at the Theatre Under the Stars in Stanley Park (he wanted to take Anne, too, but her mother would not allow it). From far away I watched a woman wearing feathers and sequins and not much else parading across the brilliantly lit stage while we huddled on the damp grass under the night sky.

Once, Anne and I got into my father's secret cache of *Playboy* magazines and laid all the centrefolds end to end across the basement floor. Of course my father was mad about it when he came downstairs and saw what we were doing, but I didn't really think it was fair of him to get so angry; he liked looking at these women, why couldn't we? For us they were a curiosity, these huge-breasted women staring boldly at the camera, they were like dolls. I would flip through the magazines and amuse myself by thinking which of the women were the prettiest: the porcelain blondes, the sultry brunettes, the perky redheads with pixie cuts.

My view of myself as a ballet dancer came to merge with my view of myself as a princess. When we played dress-up I always had to have the finest clothes. Rifling through the big cardboard box where my mother deposited her cast-off finery, I would try to decide which outfit to wear. Would it be the olive-green dress with the rucked sleeves and V-necked bodice, the evening dress with its skirt of layers of white net shot through with sequins, the black skirt with rows of ruffles that made me feel like a Spanish dancer, or the pale yellow one that ballooned out when you twirled around in it? When I had arrayed myself

in one of these costumes, I paraded down the front walk, tottering in my mother's high heels, while my friends clattered
along behind. On Hallowe'en I soon graduated from being a
witch or a ghost to being the princess in a glittery paper tiara.

*Me in my Hallowe'en tiara
in West Vancouver, 1961.*

I loved the dresses my grandmother sent, with their puffed
sleeves and the crinolines under the full skirts, and I made my
mother tie my sashes so tightly that I could hardly breathe. I
prided myself on my long hair and threatened to run away
when my father brought out the scissors to trim it.

At the costume contest in grade three I wore a wine-
coloured skirt of my mother's that shone iridescent in the sun
as I stood on the walk while she pinned a yellow rose in my
hair. I didn't win, of course, a boy with a cardboard-box TV over
him did, but I didn't care in the least. All that mattered was that
intoxicating moment of having my mother pin the rose to my
hair, the delicious scratching of the bobby pin, the fragrance of
the rose, the little rainbows dancing on the skirt.

FRIENDS

A lmost as soon as we moved to West Vancouver I discovered a neighbourhood gang of friends. There were Nancy and Jackie up the street who had television before anybody else did, Bruce next door whom I adored, Mark at the end of the block who adored me, and Karla and Linda across the street. I never felt lonely or bored. I simply went out the garden gate and there were my friends.

We played in the ditches by the side of the road where the forget-me-nots and bachelor buttons grew, and we built little bridges and sailed tiny boats in sandy streams. We climbed trees and ivy-covered stumps from the old-growth forest and built forts out of morning-glory and fir branches. In my memories it is always a sunny day in late spring or summer. My friends and I are running through the sprinkler on our lawn playing "Cowboys and Indians" or "Mother, Mother, May I," or practising handstands and cartwheels.

What I liked best of all was exploring "the creek" that ran along the bottom of a forested ravine at the end of the lane. On a hot summer day I loved plunging into the darkness of those woods, feeling the dry and springy earth on the soles of my bare feet as we ran past our castle, the worn stump of an old-growth tree crowned with a jagged peak like a tower with a little path winding up to it. We made our way along the edge of the ravine, stumbled down the bank, and skipped across the planks we had made into a bridge leading to the path through the salmonberry bushes that took us upstream. The farther we went up the mountainside, the wilder the woods became. There were tree trunks to scramble over and log-jams in the creek. We knew there were bears that followed the creek down the mountainside, although we never ran into one. My father saw one rummaging through some garbage cans in the back lane and, thinking it was a dog, told it to shoo. He was going to chase it away until he got closer and realized his mistake. There were dark mysterious pools and tiny patches of sand at the water's edge glimpsed through the sun-dappled leaves, and miniature waterfalls where the water poured like glass over boulders and broke into foam. We might stop and build a fort in the woods, or pick orange salmonberries and tart red huckleberries, or dangle our feet in a pool that was almost deep enough to swim in. Sometimes I came to the creek alone and sat on a boulder in the stream, put my bare feet in the water, and sang to myself. Jenny was not allowed to come to the creek. She had to stay inside our yard.

SISTERS

It seems to me now that we invented characters for our children. We had them firmly set to play their parts. Cynthia was bright and diligent, sensitive, courteous, watchful. Sometimes we teased her for being too conscientious, too eager to be what we in fact depended on her to be. Any reproach or failure, any rebuff, went terribly deep with her. . . . Meg was more solidly built, more reticent – not rebellious but stubborn sometimes, mysterious. Her silences seemed to us to show us her strength of character, and her negatives were taken as signs of an imperturbable independence.

    – "Miles City, Montana," *Who Do You Think You Are?*

Me with Jenny in West Vancouver.

O ne of the most autobiographical of my mother's stories, "Miles City, Montana" is based on a true incident that was legendary in our family history. It was about the time Jenny nearly drowned when we were driving back east to see our grandparents in 1961, when I was seven and Jenny was four. "Remember the time Jenny nearly drowned," we would say and I'd see myself throwing up my hands and saying "DIS-AP-PEARED" when my parents asked me where she was, just as Cynthia does in the story, and in slow motion I'd see my father leaping over the wire fence, striding through the water and running out on the pier to where the pink ruffles of Jenny's bathing-suit bottom stuck out of the water. She had seen a comb in the deep end and jumped in after it thinking the water was shallow. She was dog-paddling when my father got to her and she'd hardly swallowed any water.

When I first read the story I marvelled at my mother's ability to capture my character. Yes, that *was* me; except for physical appearances I felt I was Cynthia and Jenny was Meg. And I thought, *how could she know I was like that,* "too eager to be what we in fact depended on her to be," and so terribly sensitive to criticism, *and how could she not want to change that*? It is hard to accept that she could recreate me in fiction exactly the way I really was, without understanding the psychological angle, without knowing how I felt. She must have known.

In families we all create characters for our children. We can't help it, it's just a dynamic that evolves, one I see with my own two boys who are so different from one another, James, the

Jenny, my mother, and me in Coeur d'Alene, Washington, from the trip when "Jenny nearly drowned," in July 1961.

intense, inventive, scientific one, and Thomas, who is intuitive, physical, social. Even to ascribe adjectives is to typecast them. Perhaps in our family our characters were more delineated than in most; my mother went as far as to say that Jenny defined herself against me. While my role was to be conscientious and good, Jenny got to be rebellious, strong-willed, independent. We had a book of fairy tales in our house we always called "The Big Beautiful Book," and on the cover was a picture of a princess with wavy blonde hair. My mother saw me as the girl on the cover, while Jenny reminded her of another character in the book, named Thumbkin, an endearing urchin who wore ragged, patchwork clothes and a funny cap. Jenny had lovely dresses too, but when she didn't want to wear one of them, she might haul out some discarded item of clothing smelling of lemon oil from the ragbag and put that on instead.

At two Jenny could name the countries on the globe, at four she played chess with my grandfather Laidlaw. Her favourite

Jenny playing chess with our grandfather, Robert Laidlaw.

colour was black ("dark black," she reminds me). When she grew up she wanted to be a train. She did not even like ice cream. These preferences were repeated in our family with something approaching awe. And while I was admirable, Jenny was adorable and cuddly, though she didn't always like being cuddled. "I did like being cuddled," she told me. "Remember when Dad played 'Storm at Sea' with us?" Yes, I do remember, I remember the howling whistling sounds he made as he rocked us to and fro on the bed. Why is it that I persist in making her into a character?

It is hard for me not to see us as a study in contrasts. While I was busy trying to please, Jenny didn't seem to care a bit about what people thought of her. I ate everything on my plate – "Think of the starving children in Korea" was my father's standard line – while Jenny refused to eat what was on her plate and subsisted mostly on milk, the one thing I loathed. While I hated being late, Jenny seemed unconcerned about getting to places on time. In the mornings before school she would stand on the dining-room table with her arms languidly outstretched as my mother dressed her, while I would be in a mad panic to get out the door. I was bright and precocious around adults; she, on the other hand, refused to speak to them at all on some occasions, and I would have to act as her translator. It could be that I expressed the drive toward the conventional in the family and Jenny stood for the unconventional, nonconformist, rebellious undercurrents, the same conflict that is reflected in so many of my mother's stories.

CHAPTER 4

"Housewife Finds Time to Write Short Stories"
1959 –1963

ANNE

M y friend Anne and I are performing a minuet on our lawn, holding our hands together high in the air and circling around each other, then stepping back and curtseying very low. I am wearing a long black taffeta skirt with rows of ruffles on it, the one like a Spanish dancer's. Jenny has found a pink fairy costume and a flapper-style headband, and she runs around us waving a peacock feather as we dance. My father has dragged our record player out onto the front steps to provide the music and now sits appreciatively in a deck chair to watch our performance from the terrace above us, and applauds enthusiastically at the end.

Anne was my best friend at school. Everything about her was refined and English. She had long brown hair like me and she had a delicate bone structure and eyes that tilted up a little at the corners, giving her a gamine look, like Audrey Hepburn. At the dinner table at home my father liked to talk about Anne, about how pretty she was, about her quaint

English accent. She was a ballet dancer, too, and I compared her aristocratic feet, with their high arches, to my own broad peasant feet. It occurred to me that Anne was possibly more feminine, perhaps even prettier, than I was.

Anne lived with her mother and grandmother in an apartment in a house near Dundarave. At her house we looked at books from England, called *Andy Pandy*, and fashioned little cones of paper into medieval headdresses for her dolls. Her mother worked in an office, and when she came home she would have to lie down in the bedroom because she had a headache. On Saturdays Anne's grandmother would serve us a boiled egg and Marmite on toast for lunch. The Marmite looked like tar and tasted bitter. It was something only English people could like.

Anne James, me, and Jenny dancing a minuet in July, 1962. The little house that my father built for us is in the background.

LIPSTICK

Today Wendy is taking us to the beach. Wendy is our babysitter. Her dark hair is backcombed on top and she wears pale pink lipstick on her full lips. She is thirteen, or maybe fourteen years old. At the beach we sit on the grass near the crowded wading pool and I notice that the water looks suspiciously yellow. Jenny won't go in. Lying with my head buried in the grass I'm aware of the smell of chips and vinegar from the concession stand, which I will always associate with beaches in summer, and the words of a song coming from someone's transistor radio, about an *itsy bitsy, teeny weeny, yellow polka-dot bikini.* I roll over, and look down at the beach, where there are children wearing plastic swans or ducks around their middles paddling and shrieking in part of the water that is enclosed by safety logs on our side of the pier. On the other side of the pier is the open ocean. Wendy takes us out on the pier, where there is a group of teenage boys dangling their legs over the side. She knows how to talk to them; it's as if she's been doing this all her life.

When we get home she takes me into my parents' dark bedroom and gets me to stand in front of the mirror. She backcombs my long hair so it stands out like a lion's mane, and applies her pale pink lipstick to my mouth. I look at my tanned face, my golden brown hair, and I like what I see. It's an initiation of sorts, the beginning of a new awareness.

DAPHNE

"When I was in Vancouver in the fifties, it was like an underground society of female friendships that were totally

sustaining. All the interesting conversations – and not just
personal, but about books and everything – and all the wit –
and all the subversiveness, came from women."
– from an interview with Stephen Scobie,
Monday Magazine, November 19–25, 1982

I have photographs taken at one of the parties my parents gave, those parties in the fifties where the women wore low-cut dresses and heels and the men wore suits and ties and my father mixed old-fashioneds (rye whisky with brown sugar, Angostura, and a maraschino cherry) while I passed the peanuts. They remind me of those evening get-togethers in "Mischief" that are never over soon enough, as far as Rose is concerned. There's one of a woman sitting on the arm of a chair, a cigarette poised in her long fingers. With her hair drawn back in a French roll and her pale creamy skin, she looks a little like Maria Callas.

The woman is Daphne Cue, the friend of my mother's who lived down the lane with her husband Vic and her baby daughter Diana. My mother had many women friends in West Vancouver. There was Mari, the librarian, who'd done brilliantly at school, Lois who was left-wing and intellectual, and Deirdre, who was literary and animated, and also friends with Daphne. These were all friends who were sustaining, and not like "the Monicas," but Daphne is the one I remember best. She had moved into the neighbourhood in 1958 when Diana was still an infant. She and my mother were introduced soon afterwards but did not become friends until June of 1959, just after Jenny was born.

The woman I saw at the parties did not appear to be the same person who sat at our kitchen table and laughed her rich, honeyed laugh and talked about herself and her relatives as a source of endless drama and amusement. Her sophisticated looks did not match her personality at all. It was as if she were only impersonating an adult, as if somehow, miraculously, she had managed to come through into adulthood with the hilarity and mockery and clear vision of adolescence intact, and she was still a girl. And my mother was like this, too, at least when she was with Daphne. Even now they are like this when they are together, giddy, like Del and Naomi in *Lives of Girls and Women.*

Daphne Cue, my mother, me, and Jenny in July 1962.

Recently the three of us had lunch together, and at first I didn't recognize Daphne because she has white hair now, but she was just as beautiful, sitting next to my mother in the lobby of the Buchan Hotel in Vancouver. Their two white heads are bent together and they are engaged in an animated conversation punctuated by bursts of laughter that remind me of the laughter of teenage girls, with its edge of hysteria. All through lunch I have the same reassuring feeling that I had sitting at the kitchen table in West Vancouver, as if the adult world isn't serious after all.

They talked about someone they knew in West Vancouver whom they called "Difficult Passage." She earned this nickname because her stodgy husband had told them that in giving birth she had suffered "a difficult passage." They would sit on a log and watch this woman coming down the street and make up stories about her sex life with Mr. Difficult Passage involving such things as woolly underwear on the wedding night. Daphne said that going for a walk with my mother was "always an adventure" and that she was always making up "outrageous stories about the neighbours."

Daphne told me they had to ration their time together because my mother was spending part of each day writing. Once every two weeks they would get together and spend the whole afternoon at our kitchen table talking. "We drank enormous amounts of coffee, smoked like chimneys, and got so keyed up, talking a mile a minute." Sometimes I sat at the table with them while they drank coffee and smoked cigarettes (my mother never did learn to inhale and she would brush the ash against the side of the ashtray rather than tapping it in expertly, the way Daphne did) and listened to the river of talk that flowed between them, feeling privileged to be part of this female intimacy. They discussed the books they were reading (Daphne recalls that my mother had read "just about everything"), long biographies and nineteenth-century novels, and they talked about the characters in the books as if they were just as real as people they knew. They also told each other stories about their lives. Daphne talked a lot about someone named Bunny (her sister), and her Cape Breton relatives, and they would do imitations of their accents. Daphne said that my mother was "interested in everyone's story," and I know that more than one of Daphne's stories has made its way into my mother's fiction. The inspiration for "An Ounce of Cure" (*Dance of the Happy Shades*), in which a girl gets horribly drunk while she is babysitting and then tops off the family's liquor bottles with water before they come home, came from Daphne's story about being jilted by a high-school sweetheart. "Forgiveness in Families" (*Something I've Been Meaning to Tell You*) spun itself out of another of Daphne's stories about her family.

Of course Daphne didn't need to write the stories down; it was satisfying for her just to tell them, and in this way she was fundamentally different from my mother. I have friends like this in my own life and I find it intriguing, the way some people are able to tell marvellous stories about people's lives, but feel no need to do anything more with the material. Why is this? Why did my mother have to wrestle with the stories, to shape and render them into fiction, while Daphne did not? The simple answer is that she was an artist, and as an artist she cultivated a huge detachment; she was looking at everything from a distance and was always trying to get a larger vision.

Also, I think Daphne would be the same person no matter who she was with, while my mother, by contrast, was much more of a chameleon and could change her personality to fit whoever she was with. So often she has spoken of how she was skilled in the art of deception, of how she lived the surface everyday life and also the other "real" life of her writing. She told me that in those days she didn't really have a self. And yet Daphne described her as the "most honest and unpretentious person she ever met." Paradoxically, she had to be deceptive with most people, accommodating herself to their reality, so she could remain the observer, so she could be honest and truthful in her writing. She didn't have to do this with friends like Daphne, whose irony and mockery and non-acceptance of the status quo were compatible with her own view of the world.

MARRIED LIFE

I 'm looking at a photograph taken in 1962, of my parents and their friends the Browns before they go out to a New Year's Eve costume ball. My father is Henry VIII and looks quite the part, having unaccountably put on weight that year, perhaps

Trudy Brown, Ron Brown, my mother, and my father before a New Year's Eve party, 1962.

because he had given up cigarettes, and my mother is a Spanish dancer with a black lace shawl, called a mantilla, draped over her hair. Lean and dark, Ron Brown is a convincing Abraham Lincoln, while his wife Trudy is a flapper in a beaded dress.

The next photo: a night at the opera. My mother is wearing a black sheath dress, and the mink stole my grandfather had made up for her out of some pelts he'd saved after the demise of his mink and fox farm. I used to bury my face in the silky fur and smooth my hand over the satin lining smelling of Evening in Paris perfume. She is holding a pair of gloves, and though you can't see them, I'm imagining she has on the amethyst earrings I had given her for her birthday the year before. My father had taken me downtown to the Persian Arts and Crafts store and I had looked through one tray after another of sparkling jewellery before finally choosing those earrings. When we paid

My father and mother dressed for the opera in 1963. My mother is wearing the special mink stole she received from her father.

for them, the owner put a tiny vial of sandalwood-essence oil wrapped in tissue paper into the bag. My father beside her is thin again and boyish in spite of the suit and tie. The picture was taken by my Laidlaw grandfather, who was out from Wingham for a visit, before the three of them went to see a production of *Aida* at the Queen Elizabeth Theatre. Understandably, in this era when having a mink stole was such a status symbol, my grandfather took a professional interest in the quality of the furs the women were wearing.

Not a photo, a memory: we are sitting at the kitchen table before breakfast. My parents have been arguing and my mother picks up a plate and flings it at my father, except she tosses the plate slowly and without conviction and he ducks from the path of its wobbly flight. It hits the wall behind him.

My mother and father fought often. The kind of fights they had were not over practical things like money, or how to raise the children, or which house to buy. (My mother was easygoing and went along with most things.) Their fights were philosophical and political, representing irreconcilable world views. I'm reminded of the comment Kath makes in "Jakarta" about it being important to argue, at least with your husband, to resist going under. You had to prove you weren't intellectually inferior, because all the popular Freudian psychology was saying that you were, that women were biologically incapable of logical or abstract thinking. I'm reminded of the episode in *Lives of Girls and Women* where Del has read an article about how men look at the sky and think of the universe, while women look at the sky and think, "I have to wash my hair." It was important to be rational, to be logical, those were important virtues at that time, "masculine" virtues, whereas now it is the reverse, and the "feminine" virtues of empathy and intuition are more highly regarded than reason. In my mother's fiction there are male characters who will ask wives and girlfriends if they are premenstrual; Patrick asks this of Rose when she breaks off their engagement. My father did ask my mother this question at those times when he found her moody and volatile, "ready for battle," as he put it.

In the arguments, my father was on the side of conformity, conventional values, and conservative politics, and my mother was on the side of individualism, left-wing politics, and rebellion against conventional values. My mother thinks he did a very brave thing in marrying her and going against his parents, but that at some level what he wanted was for my mother to be the kind of conventional woman that his parents would have preferred him to marry – and he wanted the artist he did get.

My mother told me about one of these arguments. "We had a huge fight over the movie *Room at the Top* where Simone Signoret, a wonderful mature woman with intelligence and charm, is discarded for an heiress (Heather Sears), who is pretty and 'cute.'" He thought Laurence Harvey did the right thing in choosing the young girl and rejecting a woman considerably older than himself. My mother thought it was terrible. "That made me really mad. He liked the girl from the lovely background." And of course that is what he didn't get with her.

It was the kind of attitude that infuriated her. Because they almost always agreed when it came to literary opinions, and because he was a big supporter of the arts and a huge fan of her work, she found it hard to accept that his views could be so different from hers on other matters. And while she may have been above reproach as a writer in his eyes, there was an underlying rejection of her class and her background as something shameful. He corrected her Huron County accent and he

treated the Wingham relatives who came to visit with scorn
and even refused to speak to them on occasion; after his sister-
in-law Sheila came out for a visit, my grandmother, Anne
Laidlaw, complained in a letter that Jim hadn't been "one bit
nice." The story "Connection" (*The Moons of Jupiter*) draws on
similar family tensions when the narrator's lawyer husband
gives her brash, unsophisticated Cousin Iris a chilly reception
when she comes to visit, and doesn't even offer her a ride to the
bus depot afterwards.

HOUSEWIFE FINDS TIME TO WRITE SHORT STORIES

The years after we moved to the house in West Vancouver
were very difficult ones for my mother. Now in her late
twenties and a mother of two, her sense of herself as a writer was
at its most precarious. On the surface she appeared to be doing
well. In 1956 *Chatelaine* magazine bought three of her stories:
"Good-By Myra," "How Could I Do That?" and "The Dangerous
One." Robert Weaver was accepting her stories for the radio
program *Anthology*, and despite his initial reservations, "Thanks
for the Ride" came out in the second issue of *The Tamarack
Review* (Winter 1957). Yet most of these stories had been written
in the period before we moved to West Vancouver; after the
move her output dropped off considerably.

A newspaper article from the summer of 1961, the summer
she was thirty years old, ran with the memorable headline
"Housewife Finds Time to Write Short Stories." The piece
confirms that she was establishing a literary reputation, but
also hints at the frustration she was experiencing. "The
attractive young housewife and mother also finds time to write

short stories which have been widely published and broadcast. Toronto newspaper critic Robert Fulford has described her as 'the least praised good writer in Canada.' . . . Her reputation as a writer of great talent and promise has grown with each story published. . . . Until recently, however, her output has been very small because of the demands of home and family. . . . 'I've just started writing again,' she said, 'but I have to get it done during the day in between many interruptions. I work in my bedroom just snatching moments between looking after the children and the house.'"

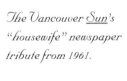

The Vancouver Sun's "housewife" newspaper tribute from 1961.

AUTHORESS Mrs. Alice Munro is pic-
tured in the garden of her home at 2749
Lawson, West Vancouver, with her   daughters Sheila (left), aged seven, and
four-year-old Jennie. Photo by Mott
Farrow.

"Least Praised Good Writer"

Housewife Finds Time
To Write Short Stories

By MOIRA FARROW

Looking after a husband, | story to Robert Weaver of | few years time—or if we mov
two small children and a house | CBC and it was broadcast on | elsewhere—I shall start wri
the radio series "Canadian | ing about B.C."
Mrs. Munro sold her first |

Her inability to write wasn't as much about the housework and the demands of motherhood as one might think. Undeniably, having two children to look after did make the logistics of writing that much more difficult than before, even though Jenny was an easy, undemanding baby. "You could give her a pencil," my mother marvelled, "and she would look at it for two hours." Finding time to write, carving out large blocks of time alone when she wouldn't be interrupted, was always a challenge, but not impossible. My father helped out by taking us on long outings on his days off, perhaps to Stanley Park, with its polar bears and penguins, its pony rides, and the little train that took us through the woods, or to one of the many beaches on Vancouver's shores. But I don't think he ever washed the dishes or changed a diaper. Men of his generation just didn't do those things.

It wasn't so much motherhood itself as the constant juggling of the roles of wife, mother, and hostess with her writing that was getting to be too much. Sustained interruptions, periods of time when she couldn't do any writing at all, were especially damaging. When her in-laws came out to visit from Oakville in the summer of 1958, one of several trips they made to the coast, she put aside her writing in order to entertain them, and it got to the point where she was almost frantic with frustration, afraid she would never write again. After that summer her sense of identity as a writer came close to collapse. Often she would sit down at her typewriter and not be able to write more than a sentence or two; she'd spend the rest of the day in a morose state of inactivity. I would come home from school and she would have done hardly any writing, or even any house-work, and it was clear she wasn't accomplishing anything.

After a time she stopped writing altogether and then she developed an ulcer (ulcers and nervous breakdowns seemed ubiquitous in the fifties). I remember how she had to drink milk, which she hated, and eat bland food because of it. She started having panic attacks, and she began suffering from a

All three grandparents at our house in West Vancouver
in May 1963. Back row: Arthur Munro, Robert Laidlaw,
Margaret Munro, my mother. Front row: Jenny, me.

bizarre anxiety disorder where she was actually afraid she would stop breathing, she literally couldn't trust that one breath would lead to another, and she was prescribed tranquillizers.

There were a number of setbacks in her writing career at this time that could have contributed to the state she was in. There were rejections of her stories, though of course rejections were nothing new. Robert Weaver went as far as to say that one of her stories, "The Cousins," was a "disastrous failure," though in the same letter he adds, "I am convinced you are one of the few really interesting writers of short stories to appear in Canada in the past half-dozen years." Fiction editor Gladys Shenner left *Chatelaine* and the new editor didn't accept any more of her stories, though this wasn't such a blow because at about the same time an editor at *The Montrealer* began to pick up on her work.

In 1958, at the urging of Robert Weaver, she applied for a Canada Council grant, and was turned down. Weaver encouraged her to contact the distinguished writer and critic George Woodcock in Vancouver for a letter of recommendation to better her chances. She couldn't phone him, so she wrote a letter, but in the end confided to Weaver, "I simply couldn't send it." Later, she speculated that the grant application was turned down because she said she needed the money for babysitting, and that if she'd said she needed it to go to Greece or something equally exotic, she would have been approved.

When I asked her about how these setbacks affected her she told me her depression didn't really have much to do with any of them. What was happening was a more internal failure of confidence that had concerned the writing itself and her identity as a writer. "I didn't feel anything good was coming from me. I felt my own gift hadn't developed and maybe wouldn't." At thirty, she felt that she was finally growing up and having to accept that some full-blown masterpiece wasn't going to burst forth of its own accord. Earlier she had been coasting along on her own virtuosity, buoyed up by what she could accomplish. Now, with maturity, she had reached an impasse; there was just too great a gap between what she wanted to write and what she was capable of writing at that time. She realized there wasn't going to be any sudden breakthrough where the writing would get easier, that it was always going to be very precarious, and very hard work, in her words, "a series of impossible leaps." Was this period in her life perhaps a necessary transition where her unconscious mind was getting ready for the leap from writing stories that she wasn't very happy with, to producing the kind of stories she really wanted to write? And could she have been in that gloomy state of inactivity others have experienced, a fallow period just before a higher level of creative expression becomes possible?

She had given up writing stories and was working on a novel

(then, much more than now, novels were considered a more worthy, more important form of literature than mere short stories). In a letter to Weaver from January 4, 1959, she reported: "I don't seem to think along short-story lines anymore. Jim wishes I did. It was much nicer financially." By the end of that year she was telling him, "the kids and I have had quite a seige of the flu. . . . I am working again after a period of considerable depression and uselessness this fall." She kept saying she was working again, but it wasn't until 1961 or 1962 that she was truly over this period of doubt and stagnation. At this time she had to admit that the novel she was working on, called *The Norwegian* or *Death of a White Fox*, was going nowhere. She sent some of her stories through Weaver to McClelland and Stewart in 1961, with the idea of having them published in a collection. Jack McClelland wrote her a letter saying that although he had the highest regard for her work, he didn't think a collection of stories would sell unless they could publish a novel of hers first.

My father took action to help her get over her writer's block. Unlike the husband in "The Office" (*Dance*), who replies to his writer wife's self-righteous speech about how she needs an office by saying only, "Go ahead, if you can find one cheap enough," my father was the one who came up with the idea of my mother renting an office. He went scouting around down in the shopping area at Dundarave and soon found a suitable location for her. Ironically, "The Office," the one story she was able to write there, is about a woman who rents an office so she can write, only to find herself being interrupted by an intrusive landlord who brings gifts she doesn't want, drops by for a chat, even secretly reads her work when she isn't there, all the while sabotaging her attempts to establish herself as a woman who dares to be a writer. While she tries to hold her ground, his campaign of harassment escalates until finally she is driven from the office just so she can be rid of him. There really was a landlord like that. My mother listened to his complaints, wrote the story, and sat in her office for another four months without writing anything more. She was waiting for some great work to burst forth and she saw the story as an intrusion, as the landlord was an intrusion, something she would set down before the real work began.

Perhaps the point of the story is that women writers must fight against some hostile presence that is censoring them and not giving them permission to write freely. Virginia Woolf has written about this sense the woman writer has, of the shadow of the Angel in the House – the Victorian ideal of a woman who is self-sacrificing, good, and pure – peering over her shoulder, forcing her to write in a conventional, constricted way. What you must do, she says, is first kill the Angel in the House and then tell "the truth of your own experience as a body." Woolf did not think she had succeeded in this second task, and she did not think any woman writer had yet succeeded, because the obstacles were so tremendous. I think my mother was struggling with these challenges when she was writing "The Office" – how not to tell the nice, conventional, moral story and, in its place, how to tell the truth of her experience as a woman. Of course she did succeed brilliantly later on, but it was very, very hard work to get there.

TRANSITION

In the summer of 1961, after we returned from our car trip back east to visit my grandparents in Oakville and my grandfather in Wingham (my grandmother had died of Parkinson's disease in 1959), my mother wrote three stories, all later included in *Dance of the Happy Shades*: "A Trip to the Coast," a story she never liked because the characters in it were so nasty, "Dance of the Happy Shades," about the Down's syndrome child who astonishes the assembled gathering at Miss Marsalles's piano recital (inspired by a dinner-table conversation in Oakville where the Munro sisters spoke about a music teacher they had had), and "The Peace of Utrecht," another breakthrough story that came out of an incident on the trip where her grandmother got out her mother's clothes to see if she wanted any of them. She had never been able to use personal material in that way before.

In a letter included with the copy of "The Peace of Utrecht" she was sending him, she told Weaver, "I have lots of ideas now but the experience of feeling so fertile after the long drought has made me uncertain about criticism. I mean I can't criticize myself very well." She knew there was something different about these stories, but she didn't necessarily believe she could ever write others like them, and she was still suffering from an enormous loss of confidence.

"It wasn't a breakthrough that I could use and I really can't explain what happened to me the next year. It was probably simply finally becoming mature and realizing that this writing thing that I had counted on was not going to come by any miracle; that the kind of writing I could do was not going to be transformed into the kind of writing I wanted and something was going to have to happen."

By the early sixties my father was growing dissatisfied with his job at Eaton's, where, after twelve years, he was still only the assistant manager of the fabric department, and was growing more frustrated with the way the organization worked, the way it didn't seem to reward innovation or invite change. He had never liked the "chumminess" at Eaton's; he never played golf with co-workers; anyone who knows him will tell you he was never a team player.

In these years my father painted and sketched. He played the French horn and listened to his records and watched *Don Messer's Jubilee* and *Sergeant Bilko* on television. He built us a playhouse in the corner of the garden and did cement work, and he cleared out the basement when it flooded. After quitting cigarettes, he took up smoking a pipe and his tweed jackets always smelled of the package of Amphora pipe tobacco he kept in the pocket. He read Philip Roth, J.D. Salinger, John Updike, and *Playboy* magazine. Briefly, he tried writing satirical essays, which I don't believe he sent anywhere. I remember seeing the typewriter out on our dining-room table, looking bold and assertive out of its usual place in the bedroom.

On the trip back east he and my mother had talked about the fantasy of having a bookstore. It was an idea he'd had back in university, to run a kind of cultural centre selling books and classical records, but the idea was all but forgotten once he married and started raising a family. After the trip, he got involved in a bookstore enterprise named Pic-a-Pocket, run by friends of theirs, Elsa and Stephen Franklin, helping them out on a volunteer basis. Paperbacks were really coming into their own at this point, hence the name Pic-a-Pocket. My father said that the book business had been run by "little old ladies of both sexes," but that with the introduction of mass-market paper-backs, that was all beginning to change. One of Pic-a-Pocket's stores was down in Dundarave; other branches were opening in suburban locations outside the downtown core. My father didn't agree with their methods; he thought one centralized location was a better idea for a bookstore, a store more like Duthie's, which had just opened in downtown Vancouver and was lending greater respectability to the book trade. As time went on he began more and more to think of opening his own store, only it could not be in Vancouver, because of Duthie's. It would have to be somewhere else.

CHAPTER 5

My Grandfather in Wingham

When I was eleven years old, my mother, my sister Jenny, and I took the CPR train "back east," a trip that took three days and four nights. We stayed in the house in Wingham, the house my mother grew up in, where my grandfather still lived, and in Oakville with Grandmom and Granddad Munro. I had purchased a red straw hat for the occasion and was feeling very grown up. I remember the huge CPR station in Vancouver and our trip up the Fraser Canyon, through tunnels and over trestles, that first night, and then the next morning seeing the Rocky Mountains from the dome car. I loved the train, with its plush seats that faced each other and were folded down and made into bunk beds at night by the black porters, with a curtain for privacy and a little ladder to the upper berth. I loved it when the three of us made the trek to the dome car, passing between cars, where the creaking and chugging of the train became so much louder, inhaling the smell of oiled metal and the sudden blast of summer heat. I enjoyed being jostled from side to side, and the slight element of danger, before entering the hush of the next car and making our way down the carpeted aisle in single file. I remember the flat expanse of the Prairies and then the small lakes and scrubby forest of the Canadian Shield that seemed to go on forever, and then coming out into fields and towns before reaching the outskirts of Toronto and finally pulling into Union Station.

Jenny, my mother, and me (with my new hat) before our train trip back east in 1965.

For me, coming from the West Coast, familiar with rainforest and mountains and ocean, the cultivated landscape of rural Ontario was exotic. From the tall brick farmhouses to the giant elm trees in the fields, to the golden crops, to the stands of hardwood trees beyond rolling hills, all of it was new and yet familiar. I ran through the tall stalks of corn in my grandfather's field and lay down on the earth and gazed up at the cloudless sky. I pumped water from the well in front of the house, inspected the barn, listened to the warm breeze in the silver maples. The heat in the evening was another novelty, and the sound of crickets, and so was the blackness of night when I lay in bed wondering how I could know I hadn't gone blind.

By this time my grandfather was raising turkeys, and he took me with him once to the turkey barn. He opened the door and I was hit by a suffocating hot smell and the squawking of hundreds of doomed birds packed together in a sea of white feathers and trembling wattles. The turkeys were a curiosity for me, partly because I found them repulsive; on another occasion, this time on my own, I opened the door of a small shed near the barn where the maimed and deformed turkeys were housed. There were birds limping on twisted legs, or listing sideways because they had only one wing; one, I remember, strutted around

A gathering of the generations of Laidlaws at Wingham, 1965. Back row: Robert Laidlaw (grandfather), my mother, Mrs. Bannerman (housekeeper), Robbie Folkard (cousin), Sheila Folkard (my mother's sister). Middle row: Aunt Maud (my mother's great-aunt), me (too good for the company). Front row: Jenny, Sarah Code (great-grandmother), Peter Folkard (cousin).

determinedly with its head on backwards, fixing me with a baleful eye.

The place I liked best was the river that ran along the border of the farm. This was the Maitland River, which was not at all like the creek of my own childhood explorations, but wide, shallow, and lethargic, like the mythical Wawanash River (sometimes called the Peregrine after Sir Peregrine Maitland) in my mother's fiction. In the hot afternoons Jenny and I tried to catch frogs in the muck and weeds near the bank (just as Del and her brother Laird do in *Lives of Girls and Women*), the cool mud sucking at my toes, or I pushed her and my cousins, Peter and Robbie, Aunt Sheila's children, upstream and down in a flat-bottomed boat I'd discovered by the edge of the bank.

My cousins, Robbie and Peter, with Jenny and me at the Maitland River.

Sometimes my grandfather came down to the river to fish. Wading into the muddy water in his high rubber boots, he swung the rod over his head in circles before casting the line out towards the middle the stream. I could tell by watching him that the way he cast the line was very important to him and that he was careful about doing it correctly. But he didn't catch anything that day, and I had the feeling he usually didn't catch anything, and the fish he did catch another day looked grey and unappetizing anyway. When he was changing out of his boots on the bank I saw there were lumpy blue veins bulging under the white skin of his legs.

Near the end of his life, when he was already in his seventies, my grandfather wrote a memoir, *Boyhood Summer, 1912*, about fishing and exploring the creek that ran behind his home. In it, he described that same procedure of casting that I watched him perform so many years later. "You have to wade out up to your waist, then to cast you whirled the hook and bait in a small circle and threw it like the South American lasso, the bolo." He and his friend Hardy spent idyllic days fishing for black bass with a bamboo pole in the "crick" and frying up their catch on its banks like Tom Sawyer.

The "crick" was the Blyth Creek that ran for miles through the dense hardwood woodlots behind the farms of Morris Township before flowing into the Maitland River. It was a wild, untamed place in those days, where my grandfather could walk for miles through the bush without ever seeing a farm, observing "the flash and chatter of a kingfisher or the scream of a giant fishhawk, or the croak of a crane flapping his big, dark, blue wings, reflected in a wavy shadow in the water," or spot deer and otter and foxes in the bush, or catch sight of a tiny weasel "whose bright fearless eyes shone among the red berries." Here, he could wander among woods of cedar and elm and maple, and come across banks of gold and green marigolds where "the pools of water between reflected green and gold and the sunlight merged everything into something like a tapestry."

(Reading these passages, I am reminded of my mother's lyrical descriptions and her unerring sense of place. She told me once that the idea for a story often came from an image of a place she remembered, something as simple as an avenue of maple trees bordering a country lane.)

On that trip when I was eleven I sensed a complicated sadness about my grandfather that merged into an image of him coming in from the barn and eating porridge alone (this was years after his wife had died and before Etta, who was to become his second wife, came into his life). There was an air of resignation about him, covered over with dignity, which had to do, I think, with a failure in the end to find any refuge. I was so affected by this vision of him having to have breakfast on his own that I even spoke to my mother about it, and when she told him about my concerns he was highly amused, shrugging off any hint of pathos or self-pity about his life.

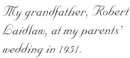

My grandfather, Robert Laidlaw, at my parents' wedding in 1951.

BOYHOOD AND YOUTH — A DOUBLE LIFE

R obert E. Laidlaw was an only child, and in his memoir he
spoke of leading a "double life" in childhood (the same
phrase my mother used when referring to her "ordinary" life as
a wife and mother, and the other life of her writing, and the
title chosen by Catherine Sheldrick Ross for the biography of
my mother she wrote for the Canadian Biography series in
1992). Like his daughter, he created a rich imaginary life from
books that filled his solitary childhood world. One part of him
lived in the world of adventure stories like *Robinson Crusoe*,
Tom Sawyer, *Treasure Island*, and tales from Greek and Roman
history with their "stirring accounts of campaigns and battles,
of sieges and slaughter, of the bravery of Leonidas and the bril-
liance of Hannibal," while the other part of him inhabited the
much less satisfying world of home and school and community. Both his parents read a good deal also, but they did not
talk about what they were reading. In this Presbyterian farming
community driven by the work ethic, "readers were viewed
with suspicion."

Growing up in the early years of the century, Robert tried
very hard to fit into the world around him. It was a world of
largely Scottish Protestant settlements, which, after the initial
burst of pioneer adventure, had settled down to a complacent
and narrow society of hard-working, church-going farmers and
townspeople who were generally not very tolerant of change or
new ideas. Despite his efforts, for the sensitive, bookish child,
Huron County was an alien and unforgiving place, as baffling
as a foreign country he had landed in where people spoke a
language he could not hope to understand. In her essay about
her parents, "Working for a Living," from the anthology

Fathers, my mother repeats a story he told about his school days as a joke. At school he learned to recite a poem that went like this:

> *Liza Grayman Ollie Minus*
> *We must make Eliza Blind.*
> *Andy Parting, Lee Behinus*
> *Foo Prince on the Sansa Time.*

Later he was startled to see the poem written on the blackboard:

> *Lives of Great men all remind us*
> *We must make our lives sublime*
> *And departing, leave behind us*
> *Footprints on the sands of time.*

My grandfather did not expect his world to make sense. He did not expect it to be rational or coherent, and he didn't question things, he just did his best to endure and to adapt, the classic Laidlaw pose.

His mother had been Sarah Code, known in her youth as the best-looking woman in the county, though in photographs it is clearly her younger sister Maud who is the true beauty in the family. Sarah, or Sadie, as she was called, was the eldest of four sisters from an Irish family. They were Anglicans, and more free and easy than their Presbyterian neighbours. Her father had been a legendary drunkard in his youth and the family had come to Morris Township to get the father away from his drinking cronies. Once she married, Sadie compensated for her background by becoming more strictly Presbyterian than her Presbyterian husband.

My mother with her great-grandfather, the once-notorious Thomas Code.

As a girl Sadie wore her rippling auburn hair in a plait over one shoulder. She grew up to be tall with an erect bearing and she was terribly proud of her tiny waist, which she maintained by drinking a glass of warm water before every meal to curb her appetite. She did not dress with confidence like her sister Maud. In "Winter Wind," in the collection *Something I've Been Meaning to Tell You*, my mother described a photograph I have of the four sisters, noting that Sadie's dress was flouncy and ridiculous while Maud's black jet outfit was much more successful. In that photograph the mother and father are seated in unsmiling Victorian rectitude, with the four daughters standing in a row behind them.

On that same trip back east in the summer of 1965, my mother and I visited my great-grandmother and my great-aunt Maud, who were living together in Wingham after their husbands had died. (Aunt Maud had been very happily married, which everyone commented on because it was so unusual.) Their

The Code sisters. Sarah, my great-grandmother, is on the left with the braid.

house had a verandah and a wooden staircase in the front hall with a curved bannister gleaming with polish. In their parlour the backs of the plush couches and armchairs were draped with anti-macassars they had crocheted, making intricate patterns of loops and knots out of the coarse white thread with the little crochet hook (also described in "Winter Wind"). They embroidered too, filling in the borders of linen napkins with leaves and flowers, and pieced together patchwork quilts from worn-out clothes, sewing the squares of fabric together with tiny, even stitches.

They were very old ladies by then, both in their eighties. (Sadie would die a few years later at the age of eighty-nine, while Maud lived on in an institution for years and years and, like the woman Rose sees when she takes Flo to the nursing home in "Spelling," could spell out words long after all her other capacities had gone.) My great-grandmother had trembly jowls and wore her hair swept up loosely on her head with a strand of auburn still visible at the top. While she was getting ice

*Great-aunt Maud
and Great-Grandmother
(Sarah Code) in the 1980s.*

cream for us in their kitchen I sat at the dining-room table and
stared at the wedding photo on the wall, marvelling at that tiny
waist in the Edwardian dress. Then I looked over at the sacklike
figure in the kitchen in the shapeless housedress, with bulges
and hollows at all the wrong places, and no waistline at all.

Before she married William Laidlaw, Sadie was engaged to a
cousin of his, James Laidlaw, whom my mother remembers as an
exceedingly handsome old man. James made a fatal mistake
when, after he hadn't seen her for some time, he made some
comment to her about how she had put on weight. Was he insin-
uating that she was pregnant? Could she have been pregnant?
(This is the kind of speculation about the past my mother loves
to indulge in, the kind that led to a story like "Meneseteung," in
Friend of My Youth, about the Victorian poetess who spurns
her chance for marriage after discovering the half-naked,

beaten body of a woman who has been in a drunken brawl by the back fence.) For whatever reason, proud Sadie broke off the engagement and soon afterwards married William Laidlaw, the taciturn, hard-working farmer who read in the evenings and spoke to his wife and family only when necessary.

Robert was born about eleven months after their marriage and there were no children after that, a very unusual situation in those days before reliable birth control. My mother wonders about that too. Did they ever have sex after their son was born? She remembers feeling a terrible tension in that family, though in his memoir my grandfather said only that he received "a reasonable amount of love but as there was a certain fear of spoilage (*sic*) this was well tempered with discipline."

Sadie did not want her son to become a farmer like his father. She hoped he would go to university and become a professional man, a minister or a teacher, perhaps even a lawyer. Robert did very well at the one-room school down the concession road from his farm, and at the age of twelve he wrote the entrance exams that allowed him to attend the Continuation School (high school) in Blyth. But at the Continuation School something went wrong. Was it that he was younger than the other students? Or did natural Laidlaw timidity get the better of him? We do know that in 1916, when he was fourteen, he failed his exams, with an average of fifty-five per cent when he needed sixty per cent to pass, and that afterwards he dropped out and never completed his grade twelve at the Continuation School, so all possibilities for a university education and a professional career were closed to him. (My mother's situation would have been similar to his if she had not won a scholarship to go to university after grade thirteen. She spoke of how terribly difficult it was to get away from Wingham, and I can well imagine how it could have been psychologically impossible for my grandfather to make the break.)

Without any hope of getting to university, what prospect lay before Robert besides that of becoming a farmer like his father? What was to become of him? Perhaps not unexpectedly, given his individual nature, my grandfather did find a way out; he found the answer in the woods and the creek he had explored as a boy. Unlike most of his contemporaries who put aside childish *Last of the Mohicans* fantasies, Robert gravitated to the bush more after he left school, and by his late teens, while continuing to live with his parents on the farm and helping out with the chores, he was trapping and fishing in the bush that ran for miles along the Blyth Creek, catching marten, mink, otters, and foxes, and selling their pelts. He made quite a good living. In 1920, the pelt of a red fox fetched about twelve dollars, mink, eight to twelve dollars, raccoon, five to ten dollars, muskrat two dollars and fifty cents. (A worker's wage at that time was ten to fifteen dollars a week.)

In a letter written to my mother in 1961, he gave an account of his trapping life. "I would start out in October well before the season, plan out a route preferably in some sort of circle following ridges and bush. . . . The first week in November I would start out carrying a knapsack of traps" along with "a hatchet and a .22 rifle and a good knife," and walking as far as twenty or even twenty-five miles a day along the trapline. He describes the peculiarities of 'coons, muskrats, mink, and skunks and the best ways to catch each of them, and tries to capture the feeling it gave him. "There was something of a thrill to it. Perhaps it was in doing the unusual or getting back to nature or a primitive animal feeling of being part of the outdoors. Anyway I loved it at that time."

In 1925 Robert bought two silver foxes (silver foxes were actually black with an overlay of white hairs on their tails and back) and built pens for them on his parents' property. Soon, raising foxes in captivity took over from trapping in the bush. Sadie supported the enterprise; he was making a living and it allowed him to stay close to her. His father did not say what he thought.

FOX FARMER

An Irish cousin of his, Anne Clarke Chamney, who was related to him on his mother's side, came for a visit. Right away she saw a potential for making money from the fox-farming business. (Sadie thought she was feigning an interest in the foxes but my mother has written in her essay "Working for a Living" that her enthusiasm was genuine, that she was the kind of woman who thrived on business enterprises.)

At the time, Anne was nearly thirty, and the principal of a four-room school, but she still wanted a family and must have been anxious to marry. Robert was in his late twenties and, because of the Laidlaw shyness, he had not had any romantic involvements (at least not any that the family knew about) before she arrived on the scene. They married in 1927 and, with some money Anne had saved from teaching, they bought a piece of land in Turnberry Township, at the end of Lowertown Road in Wingham, and Robert invested in more silver foxes and started breeding them, and later, after about 1938, mink also.

"Boys and Girls" (*Dance*) describes the fox-farming operation in detail, the warren of pens the father builds, "like a medieval town" with its complicated system for feeding, and the faces of the foxes, "drawn exquisitely sharp in pure hostility," though my

The wedding of my mother's parents,
Robert Laidlaw and Anne Chamney, in 1927.

mother did tell me the "pelting operation" never did take place inside the house as it is described here, as permeating the whole house with "the smell of blood and animal fat, with the strong primitive odour of the fox itself." The butchering of horses for fox food was something that did occur; horses that were old or lame were kept on the farm before they were slaughtered, as they are in "Boys and Girls."

Robert worked very hard, but almost from the beginning the enterprise failed to thrive; circumstances were against him. He and Anne could not have known it, but they had entered the fox-farming business at the worst possible time, just when the demand was going down. Of course, things got much worse when the Great Depression hit a couple of years later, and the market for fox and mink furs declined even further during the War, when other people were beginning to do well again. My mother said at first there were good years and bad years, but then there were more bad years than good years. By the time the War ended, the business had begun a disastrous slide from which it would not recover. The family was so poor that they switched from wood to burning sawdust for heat, and the sawdust got all over the house.

In 1947, when my mother was sixteen, Robert took a job as a night watchman at the iron foundry in town, the Western Foundry Co. Ltd., while continuing to work during the day dismantling the mink and fox operation, tearing down pens and getting rid of his stock, saving only a few pelts, which he later had made into a mink stole for my mother.

In the mid-fifties, as a sideline, he began raising turkeys on the farm, and the new business was at least marginally successful, though it was also beset with problems – "epidemics, fires, low prices etc." as he put it in one letter. He had to continue working at the foundry for many more years, making thirty-five to forty dollars a week at this job, hardly enough to live on. (The work involved a back-breaking procedure called "shaking down floors," described by my mother in "Working for a Living," which involved lifting heavy metal casings. She thinks the work accounted for his bad heart in later years.) He kept hoping that the turkey business, which was strenuous work in itself, would be successful enough to allow him to quit the foundry. Eventually it was, but not until 1963, when he was over sixty. He often spoke of his money worries in his letters to my mother; something as basic as having his truck repaired would wipe out his plans for coming to B.C. for a visit. In later years he wrote letters to her from the foundry, complaining of how the monotony of the work was getting to him: "it is very dull here tonight at the foundry and I am feeling low."

In his adult life my grandfather was reasonably successful in creating a persona of himself as a regular farmer without pretensions or eccentricities. Most people did not know that he was quietly reading his way through all the books in the Wingham Public Library. The secrecy meant that no one could say he was putting on airs; no one mocked him. In "Working for a Living," my mother wrote, "He had a streak of pride posing as humility, making him scared and touchy, ready to bow out, never ask questions." She has described the "extraordinary timidity" of her Laidlaw relatives; she remembers visiting cousins who just sat quivering and were unable to say a word. Near the end of his life, my grandfather confessed to her that he had suffered from "a terrible shyness, that I have mostly overcome."

If he were living now he might be diagnosed as having social-anxiety disorder. He might be on Prozac. If all the relatives who were socially terrified had been on Prozac, would they have ventured forth bravely into the world? Now they would be diagnosed as having a chemical imbalance in the brain, not some shameful failure of nerve. How might that have changed their lives?

FATHER AND DAUGHTER

It was my grandfather's conflicting drives, to blend in and to stand apart, his social self-consciousness and fear of ridicule at war with his intellectual daring and scepticism, that led to his need for a double life. This was something my mother inherited from him; she was like him in temperament, with the same ability to be a "fitter inner" and yet remain a separate observer, but she was saved by an extra dash of courage that perhaps came from her mother's side. When she was a little girl, her mother would take her skating on Saturday afternoons. Young Alice could not learn to skate; she could not do physical things when anyone was watching, and for her, the skating sessions were a torment. Her mother was oblivious to what she was feeling but her father knew. He knew that she suffered, but he was not sympathetic. In my mother's words, "He did not want to know that there was another like him in the world."

When she speaks of her "long training in the art of deception," it is the example set by my grandfather she is thinking of. She has spoken often of her art for dissembling, for concealment, which, for a writer, can be very advantageous, allowing her to remain free and detached, almost without a self. When she was in university, her landlady remarked that a story of hers she had read wasn't a bit like her. Why would you expect my writing to be like me? was my mother's reply. The strategy worked for her in the fifties as well when the appearance of being an ordinary wife and mother meant that people left her alone while she got on with her work. She told me once that "the triumph of my life is that none of the environments I found myself in prevailed over me." Robert Laidlaw's daughter knew that it was very, very important never to brag, never to reveal the extent of one's ambition, never to seem better than anybody else. (To this day, my mother never tells me when she has won a literary prize or had some honour bestowed on her, or even if she's had a story published. I have to ask. Otherwise she never mentions it.) It is better to be that way than it is to blunder on, oblivious to what others are thinking, and thus appear ridiculous, as Ada does when she comes to Del's school in *Lives of Girls and Women*, or when she hosts the tea party for the ladies in town while her daughter looks on with acute embarrassment and shame.

Late in life, Robert reflected on his earlier relationship with my mother in a letter he wrote to her. "When thinking back to what I remember of our contacts when you were growing up, it seems that nothing between us was taken quite seriously, life was a subtle sort of joke. That is what I remember of you as a child and teenager, nearly always good-humoured, never bumptious. I don't recall you whinging or complaining about hard times and they sure were hard."

Four generations:
Robert Laidlaw,
me, my mother,
and Sarah Code (seated).

ETTA

By the time I visited my grandfather again, when I was seventeen, he was married to Mary Etta Laidlaw, "Aunt

Etta," the model for Irlma in the autobiographical story
"Home" (*Best Canadian Stories*, 1974). Etta had been recently
widowed after being married to a distant cousin of his, Tom
Laidlaw. Etta was loud and bossy and baked good pies. She
had a way with plants and animals and would tell you so as
she took you on a tour of the garden. She had geraniums
growing in pots on the windowsills, and successful tomatoes.
She owned a magnificent white Samoyed named Rinny and a
cat named Tom that she had "fixed" by tying an elastic band
tightly around his balls. The fact that the cat who suffered this
fate was named after her first husband was not lost on our family.

Etta smoked, and she always carried around an ashtray
with a little tin lid on it she could snap open and expertly flick
her ash into. Her short brassy hair was combed off the face
and shaved at the back of the neck, like a man's, and the
glasses she wore made her eyes look as big as a bullfrog's. In
the evenings she liked beating Jenny and me and my grandfather
at rummy and in the mornings she would yell to us up the
stairs, "Git up, ya lazy buggers," a phrase that became part of our
family vocabulary. At her cottage by Lake Huron she kept a
little mound of fake doggie doo she planted in strategic
corners so visitors would think it was the real thing. In a
letter she wrote to my mother, Etta talks about the cyclamen
plant my mother gave her that had never been without bloom in
one year and five months. Over the winter she had embroidered
a pair of pillowcases and she was knitting an afghan. Before
signing off, she included a joke. "Here's a recipe = How to
cook toilet paper. Answer = Brown on both sides and throw it
in the pot."

I think my grandfather would have felt comfortable with
someone like Etta, who was so unsophisticated compared to

him, and it suited him just fine to keep his own world of books and ideas completely separate, the way he had done all his life. He could adapt to her jokey style easily, without her even being aware how delicately his behaviour was calibrated to mesh with hers. And he would have been happy to have someone to care for him and look after him after all the years of being with a wife who was bedridden, and then being on his own.

THE MCGREGORS

Near the end of his life, when he was about seventy years old, my grandfather embarked on a writing career. He wrote historical pieces for the Blyth paper, memoirs like *Boyhood Summer, 1912*, and in the year before his death, a historical novel, *The McGregors: A Novel of an Ontario Pioneer Family*, an account of the Scottish immigrants who settled rural Ontario in the mid-nineteenth century.

My grandfather died in 1976 and the book was published in 1979. In his introduction, Harry J. Boyle (who had grown up in nearby St. Augustine before becoming a successful author and CBC producer in Toronto) called *The McGregors* "a true chronicle" of the way people lived, the way they built things, the rituals they observed.

In 1974 my grandfather wrote to my mother about what he was trying to achieve with it. "First I wanted to, in fact have to, write about the period 1850 to 1925. Next I wanted to bring out the tragedy of reticent people, not necessarily all Scottish but to know them first hand." The novel spans three generations in the lives of the McGregor family. Rory comes to Bruce County with his family in 1851; his son Black Jim works on a framing crew building barns all over the county, and eventually marries and buys his own farm. The years ahead are full of hard but satisfying work, clearing the land, building a home, sowing and harvesting the crops, and his labour is rewarded by years of contentment and relative prosperity. When Jim and his wife Janet are old, their son, John, who has fought in World War I, and his bride, Katie, take over the farm.

My grandfather writes about the lives of these early settlers with affection and respect, perhaps too much respect. What stands out most is his tremendous knowledge about pioneer life in that part of the country, so the book is filled with authentic descriptions of how things were done, from cutting down trees to building barns, to shooting partridges, to collecting maple syrup, to sewing a patchwork quilt. He describes courting rituals, what people ate and drank, even the inside of a one-room school with a portrait of Queen Victoria and a map of Africa on the wall.

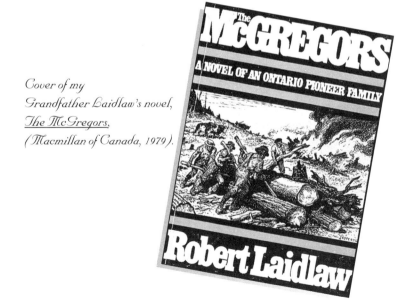

Cover of my Grandfather Laidlaw's novel, The McGregors, (Macmillan of Canada, 1979).

The McGregors also suffers from being an old-fashioned novel. For instance, the courtly attitude toward the women characters strikes the contemporary reader as patronizing. Here is John watching his bride-to-be come down the stairs. "To any eye she was a lovely sight, but to John she seemed exquisite, as far from the snub-nosed schoolgirl as a butterfly from its cocoon." Most of the time the writing skims the surface of characters, who are a little too good, a little too nice to be very interesting, and there are occasional lapses into sentimentality.

For me there was something static and unfulfilled in the way my grandfather wrote about the cycle of farming life, contentment but little sense of drama or discovery, and I suspect this is how he felt about his own life. Why would he have used the phrase "the tragedy of reticent people" if he didn't feel there was something tragic about his own life? Jim McGregor's words, "We lack something, we Scots people . . . I did not love my father and I fear my John does not love me. We are afraid to even use the word 'love' in our family," hint at my grandfather's own estrangement from his father, and the Presbyterian chill that fell over his childhood. And when she is old and looking back on her life, Janet says, "Where are the dreams we had? The dreams I had as a young girl?" I imagine my grandfather felt much the same about his own life as a fox farmer. His memoir, *Boyhood Summer, 1912*, ends on a similarly elegiac note: "I followed dreams all my life. They faded and left me with little that is definite, much that is indefinite."

Occasionally I find echoes of my mother's fiction when he hints at a darker side to the lives of these pioneers. When Janet first sees the McGregors' house, she is appalled by its austerity. "There was an uncompromising harshness that accepted no ornament, no bit of bright colour, no relief from things strictly utilitarian. Everything was clean, but it was an oppressive cleanliness that spoke of lye and homemade soap and scrub-brushes."

Similarly, in my mother's story "A Stone in the Field," part of "Chaddeleys and Flemings," my mother describes a young girl's visit to her aunts, who live out in the country, and her experience of sitting with them in the kitchen. "The room was cleaner and barer than any I have ever been in. There was no sign of frivolity, no indication that the people who lived here ever sought entertainment. No radio; no newspapers or magazines; certainly no books."

My grandfather is amusing in this satirical account of a Presbyterian church service: ". . . the service itself was almost as chilly as the air in the church, for religion was a serious business here. The lighter, sometimes smiling approach of their Methodist neighbours was frowned upon. During an interminable sermon, members of the congregation gradually gave up trying to follow the unfamiliar combination of Elizabethan English and Hebrew mythology and thought about other things. Adults, well trained, sat silently enduring, the luckier ones asleep." When the sermon is finally over "the last psalm was sung with embarrassing relief."

After he had finished the manuscript of this novel, he gave it to my mother to read. She told him she thought it needed work. In the weeks remaining before the heart operation from which he never regained consciousness, he worked with feverish intensity, seeking her advice while revising and rewriting the entire manuscript.

"I remember visiting him in the hospital about six weeks or two months before he died. He was in the Wingham Hospital and he was talking to me about the book. He was sitting up on the edge of his bed in his pyjamas. And I had read it and he talked about the characters and what he should do with them. And then he actually did write steadily from then until he died. He finished it before he went to have the operation, just finished it in time."

In the novel's closing words, when Jim McGregor is dying, my grandfather must have been foreseeing his own death. "But the darkness was coming again. It was almost there. He closed his eyes against it."

The last time I saw him, in 1975, I remember him standing in the kitchen at Wingham mopping the sweat off his fore-head with a handkerchief (his bad heart made him sweat copious amounts), talking of how, in his life, he'd "been around almost full circle." Shortly before his operation my mother showed my sister Jenny and me a sort of summing-up letter he'd sent her, mentioning how Jenny was such a tal-ented artist, and I was "a very nice person" (for him, being nice was at least as important as being talented). He must have known his chances were not good.

In "The Moons of Jupiter," Janet's father is in the hospital with a bad heart, and in this character of the father I see so much of the courtliness and dignity, irony, and philosophical nature of my grandfather. Like the father in the story, Robert initially decided against having an operation, then did an about-face, deciding at the last minute to take a chance. I can imagine him confiding in my mother the way this character does when he says, "The trouble was I was always afraid to take chances." And I see my mother's relationship with him in the way the narrator describes her father. "Whenever I told people about my father I stressed his independence, his self-sufficiency, his forbearance. He worked in a factory, he worked in his garden, he read history books. He could tell you about the Roman emperors or the Balkan wars. He never made a fuss." That is how I see my grandfather, the kind of man who would quote poetry, but always with "a scoffing note in his voice, to excuse the showing-off and the pleasure"; the kind of man whose last conversation with his daughter could well have been about naming the moons of Jupiter. I'm reminded of my mother in Janet's "appalling rush of love and recognition" and in her need to pull back and adopt a false jaunty tone with her father, in the way they shared an ironic sense of humour and a love of knowledge for its own sake until the very end.

CHAPTER 6

Laidlaw Pioneers

In the early evening Gerry, my mother, and I decide to go for a drive in the sleek green minivan that has recently replaced Gerry's red pickup truck. They bought it for the grandchildren, my mother told me: "Now we can be like all the other grandparents." Today we see the minivan as the solution to our problems. For one thing it has air conditioning. All day the heat has been pressing in on us with that sullen oppressive force of the Ontario summer that I had almost forgotten. Also we are hoping the drive will get my two-year-old son Thomas to sleep. Today I've been following him around and around the garden, making sure he doesn't get near the road. We've watered the flower bed, we've filled the plastic pool and gone down to the train tracks behind the house, and he's climbed into the bathtub in the backyard that's meant as a humorous sculpture.

I have always loved this countryside, the two-storey brick farmhouses with their gables and avenues of maple trees, the golden fields of wheat and corn, the woodlots still dense with hardwood trees bordering on quiet streams, a memory of wilderness. The towns look much as they did a hundred years ago: clusters of church spires, a town hall of red brick with high arched windows and a Victorian turret on the main street, a block or two away the mansions with their sweeping lawns and cultivated flower beds speaking of prosperity and rectitude on streets lined with towering maple trees shimmering silver in the breeze.

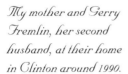

My mother and Gerry Fremlin, her second husband, at their home in Clinton around 1990.

As a child I always felt a great nostalgia for this landscape, and I took comfort in its cultivation and its human scale, so far from the wildness of the mountains, the vastness of the ocean that could not be tamed. Every time I saw this part of the country I felt I had arrived home.

My sisters are in the garden too. Andrea, the baby of the family, twelve years younger than I am, is curling Jenny's hair in the most leisurely fashion. She grasps each strand of hair with the curling iron, slowly winds it towards the scalp and holds it for a few seconds. I'm reminded of the times Jenny and I used to brush each other's hair and I can almost feel the tingling on the scalp and the gentle pulling on my long hair that left me drowsy with pleasure. Oh, to have time for that now. To be able to sip a gin and tonic on the verandah without having to leap up and follow Thomas, to be able to have an uninterrupted conversation. *How can they even imagine what having children is like?*

It's been like this every day since I arrived. There is no crib here and he does not take naps, or eat regular meals. All the routines of home have broken down. Every day I follow him around until we both collapse into bed at night. Every night I plan to get up once Thomas is asleep, and every night I fall asleep in my clothes without even brushing my teeth.

Now I see the places I visit in terms of dangers. The week before I'd been at Jenny's studio apartment in downtown Toronto. I arrived at her corner one sultry evening after taking a cab from the airport, and started to lug the stroller, my bag, and a sleeping Thomas up three flights of stairs. By the time I reached the third flight of stairs she heard me gasping for breath and came to rescue me, paintbrush in hand. Once we got settled in she showed me one of her paintings, a bird in a tree, a man walking along a road, and a building on fire in the distance. It took me a moment to realize that the man was wearing medieval dress. Many of her paintings are like this, full of mysterious incongruities. But when she got out a book on Breughel, Thomas was going into the bedroom where the fan was, and the huge mirror propped against the wall. I thought of the sharp blades of the fan, broken shards of glass, an open window and the pavement below. Breughel was set aside.

In the minivan Thomas is beside me in his car seat taking swigs from his bottle. My mother and Gerry are in the front. Gerry always drives; my mother has never learned how. I ask them about the books that influenced them the most when they were children. "I've often said that it was *Emily of New Moon* or *Wuthering Heights* but it's probably *Beautiful Girlhood*," says my mother. Then she recites part of the inscription in the book from a poem by Charles Kingsley, "'Be good sweet maid/And let who will be clever.' I thought I'd do the opposite." Gerry laughs. He insists his most influential book was *The Little Red Hen*. I tell them mine is *The Second Sex*, though I feel a little pompous in saying that.

Sitting in the back seat with Thomas sleeping beside me as I listen to their conversation, I feel more and more like a child. I have become dull and uninteresting and I can't come up with anything witty to say. I stare out the window and disappear into the landscape. I wonder absently about what the interiors of those farmhouses are like. Not enough light, I decide, the windows are too small. I picture old, stained wallpaper, cramped rooms, linoleum floors.

Suddenly I'm watching a scene from a hundred years ago. A mother, father, and son are coming down their lane in a horse-drawn buggy, all wearing black, the woman in a long dress and bonnet, the men sporting full beards under broad-brimmed hats. They are Mennonites. The fields on their farms are recognizable because in them the wheat has been stacked by hand in the shape of teepees. In one of those fields I see a man using a pitchfork to load the wheat onto a horse-drawn cart.

We drive through the town of Blyth and turn east onto one of the straight concession roads that score the rich agricultural land of Morris Township, dividing it up into neat rectangles.

After a couple of miles we come to the place where my great-grandparents' farm had been. The house is gone now and we look across an open field to the woods surrounding the Blyth Creek, the remains of the original forest that the pioneers left as woodlots to supply firewood and building materials when they were clearing the land. Further along, at a crossroads, is the one-room schoolhouse my grandfather attended as a boy. We turn down a narrow road and stop at a little bridge that crosses the creek. I am drawn to the tangle of woods on its banks and the way the trees form a canopy over the shady stream, but we don't go down to the water. There are nettles growing along the banks and my mother tells me my grandfather's beloved creek is now oozing pesticides from the farms.

Earlier I had been looking through the photographs of my Laidlaw ancestors that lie buried in an old trunk in the upstairs of my mother's house in Clinton, one of the trunks that came out from Victoria. I came across one I'd never seen before, a Victorian portrait of a man and his wife sitting side by side. The man has a broad, expansive face, a prominent nose, long whiskers, and an untamed beard. The woman has a very odd birdlike face with a pinched mouth, and thick eyebrows, and is wearing an expression I've seen on my Aunt Sheila's face. Her dark hair is parted in the middle and pulled back severely over a low forehead and tucked behind large sticking-out ears. She is wearing a dress buttoned tightly up the front, trimmed with braid, the tight bodice giving way to voluminous puffed sleeves. The couple are my mother's great-grandparents, Thomas Laidlaw and Margaret Armour. Another Thomas in the family.

My mother's great-grandparents,
Thomas Laidlaw and Margaret Armour.

THOMAS LAIDLAW

Thomas Laidlaw came as a pioneer to Morris Township from Halton County, a more settled area much closer to Toronto, in 1851, when he was fifteen years old, along with his older brother John, who was eighteen, and their cousin Robert, a little older. In a memoir written many years later, Robert described how the three "got a box of bed-clothes and a few cooking utensils into a wagon and started from the County of Halton to try our fortunes in the wilds of Morris Township." They were only the seventh family to take up land in the township, which at the time consisted largely of stands of hardwood and tangled bush with very little open space suitable for farming.

Together, they raised a log shanty, filling in the cracks with mud and moss, erecting "a big slab of elm for a door," and cutting rough planks of ash for a floor. They fashioned a "bachelor bed" out of piled hemlock branches and the three of them slept under a buffalo robe a neighbour had given them. Thomas was given the cooking and cleaning duties because he was the youngest. The story "A Wilderness Station" (*Open Secrets*) incorporates many of the details from Robert's account, as it tells the story of the two fictional brothers, Simon and George Herron, who come from Halton County to Morris Township in 1851.

The young Laidlaws went looking for work helping other settlers, but even though they were "three good-looking fellows," there were so few inhabitants in that part of Huron County there was little work to be had. Years later, when he was an old man, Thomas wrote an account of his experience, "Summer Work in the Early Fifties" by An Old Morris Boy, describing how he set out on foot in the direction of Brantford with only twenty-five cents in his pocket. By the time he got past Woodstock he was famished. "About this time I became very hungry, but as my money was all gone I was reduced to begging. I passed house after house in the attempt to work up my courage to ask for food . . . at last a school master's daughter gave me some crusts of dry bread and a big bowl of thick sour milk." Soon he did find work on some farms, "cradling, binding and drawing in the grain," and was able to return to Morris with money in his pocket before winter set in.

Thomas's mother, Mary, and sister, Jane, later came out from the farm in Halton County. That was where the extended family had been living since the death of Thomas's father, William, from cholera soon after coming out from Scotland. Jane had been born on the same day that her father died, probably from drinking the water at the Lockport Canal where he was working at the time, near the family homestead at Joliet, Illinois. Before coming out from Scotland, William Laidlaw had made an earlier move, leaving the parish of Ettrick in the Border country where he was born, heading north a hundred miles or so to work as a sheep manager in the Highlands. This was during the Highland Clearances, when the peasant farmers, the crofters, were being driven off the land they farmed and replaced by sheep. While he was working in the Highlands in 1825, and still single, William received a letter from Mary Scott, a girl he had known back in Ettrick. It was a coy letter in which Mary, after giving the news of all the weddings that had taken place, came close to making a marriage proposal:

> *"you said in your letter that you expected to hear of my weding it is not but what I might but have never thought A bout it yet or sertnly I would have wrote you and given you a invitation. I supose I will be lik the old Almaniks that no person will by soon you wrote me about comming to you which I think something hard to answer. I will not say that i will not come but perhaps I think that is A jok in your letter you say you have plenty of time for seeing the lasis you may come some moonlit night and see me which I think you would preferd befor any."* January 18, 1825.

They were married soon after William received this letter.

After William's death in Illinois, his brother Andrew (who had come to Canada some years before) made an epic journey by oxcart and took the widow and her small children back to the Halton County farm. After Mary and Jane arrived at the Morris shanty and took over the domestic arrangements, the men were free to continue clearing the land. "Aunt and Cousin had things fixed up in fine style," reported Robert. "Thomas got his discharge from baking and cooking, and we all felt the change to be for the better. We worked on, getting some of the huge trees down, but we were not much accustomed to the work and the snow was getting very deep again, the going was very slow."

Thomas and John's oldest brother James came to Morris in the fall of 1852, meaning that the little family from Joliet was reunited, and once again on their own land. But a few months later, while he was helping clear land, James was killed by a falling tree, leaving behind a wife and a baby daughter. Cousin Robert was at the scene of the accident:

"James and I went to help John with the building [of a shanty], and as we were falling a tree, one of its branches was broken in the falling, and thrown backwards, hitting James on the head, and killing him instantly. We had to carry his body a mile and a quarter to the nearest house, and I had to convey the sad news to his wife, mother, brother and sister. It was the saddest errand of my life. I had to get help to carry the body home, as there was only a footpath through the bush, and the snow was very deep and soft. This was on April 5th, 1853."

My mother has used this falling tree incident in the story "A Wilderness Station" (*Open Secrets*), though characteristically she does not take the event at face value. She has to ask: *What if? What if it hadn't been an accident? What if James had been murdered?* One of her most structurally complex constructions, the story unfolds through a series of letters and reminiscences, material uncovered by an academic who is writing a biography of a politician named Treece Herron. There is a reminiscence by the younger of two brothers, George and Simon Herron, who have come from Halton County to the district (just as Thomas and John Laidlaw did). It incorporates some of the details from Robert Laidlaw's actual account, including how the stagecoach had "quit running," how the shanty was built with its "big slab of elm for a door," even how the brothers lit a fire in the middle of the floor and nearly burned it down. My mother, however, adds a tension between the brothers, and intimates that the older one is an unbending, difficult person. She departs completely from the historical record when she has the older brother George marry a woman from an orphanage, Annie, who is the central character in the story.

"A Wilderness Station" is like one of those Russian dolls with smaller and smaller dolls inside them; here, there are stories within stories. The official story is that Simon has been killed by a falling tree, and George has had to drag the body home where he and the widowed Annie have to bury it themselves because a huge snowstorm makes travel impossible. Later Annie turns herself in at the County Gaol in Walley (Goderich), claiming that he wasn't killed by a falling tree after all, that she murdered him by smashing a rock down on his head because he beat her. Annie's story emerges in the correspondence between the local preacher, who is concerned for her welfare and doesn't believe her story for one minute, and the Clerk of the Peace at Walley. From the Gaol Annie smuggles a letter out to her old friend Sadie back at the orphanage, in which she says that it was actually George who murdered Simon, that when she was preparing the body for burial she saw the place where the axe had struck the back of his neck.

Finally, there is the correspondence from a wealthy woman the biographer has tracked down, a Miss Mullen, who employed "Old Annie" as a maid many years later. This woman remembers taking Annie to see George Herron as a very old man, at her request, and how the two old people had a private conversation, the subject of which remains hidden. It becomes clear from the anecdotes the woman relates, however, that Annie was anything but a reliable storyteller. The reader is left wondering what really happened. Who was telling the truth? How can we know the truth when all we have are the stories piled up on the rubbish heap of history? We are left sifting through the rubble.

We know that, in real life, Thomas and John stayed on in Morris Township, and their cousin Robert also settled there a few years later. They married, raised families, and built up their farms, while they witnessed the coming of the railroad and the building of roads and schools and churches and towns and saw the land being transformed from a wilderness of hardwood forest into a prosperous farming community of open fields and split-rail fences.

Thomas stayed on the farm, which he passed on to his only son William, my mother's grandfather. His brother John became restless and took his family off to British Columbia to begin the pioneering experiment all over again. The second attempt at homesteading (near Harrison Lake) was not a success, and the family moved to Vancouver, where John worked in a laundry until he was seventy-five years old.

Recently one of my mother's relatives sent her a copy of a memoir written by R.A. Laidlaw, one of John's sons. Called *Recollections of Early Vancouver*, the manuscript is based on the author's memories of downtown Vancouver between 1895 and 1910, when he was delivering laundry in the area, having gone into the same business as his father. What was remarkable to my mother about this account was the way it resurrected every building on every street, every store, every hotel, every restaurant, the way that the fictional Uncle Craig does in his voluminous chronicle of Wawanash County in *Lives of Girls and Women*. She had not known she had her own "Uncle Craig" in the family. In creating his character, she was wrestling with the problem of how to capture the past without describing every single detail, without producing something that is dead and useless, that no one wants to read. For the Laidlaws – at least for R.A. Laidlaw and for my grandfather – it was tremendously important to reconstruct the past faithfully, without leaving anything out. The challenge my mother has set herself has been to recreate history imaginatively, to give an accurate impression without recording all the details.

IN THE BLYTH CEMETERY, 1998

Today my mother, Gerry, and I visit the cemetery on a hillside just south of Blyth. We find the stone erected to the former Scottish shepherd William Laidlaw, the one who died of cholera in faraway Illinois, and his wife Mary, who later died of cholera also, in an 1868 epidemic, along with Robert's two children. Laboriously we decipher its inscription, piecing together the chiselled words eaten away by time and lichen, until we are able to read out the words of the lugubrious Presbyterian verse:

Both old and young O death, must yield to thee
And day by day thy powerful arms we see
In vain the tear, in vain the heartfelt sigh
All that are born to live are born to die.

Other Laidlaw graves are in the same row. Here lies Mary and William's daughter Jane, born in Joliet on the day of her father's death; she died in childbirth on June 24, 1866, aged 26 years. Beside her is her husband Neil, killed in an accident on

August 9, 1874, Aged 39 Years, and baby Marian, daughter of Thomas and Margaret, Died July 23rd, 1868. Aged 15 Months.

The cemetery stands as a reminder of what a chance these settlers took. So many young women died in childbirth, so many aged twenty-one or twenty-two, so many infants "only sleeping," baby angels peering out from headstones, tiny stone booties. So many young men killed in accidents. Epidemics of cholera and typhus cutting a swathe through families. What was it like to live with death so near at hand, with such a real possibility that your child would die? How did people go on with their lives? Faith, I suppose. Faith in a better world to come. Acceptance. The Lord giveth and the Lord taketh away. In vain the tear, in vain the heartfelt sigh. You got on with things.

After visiting the cemetery we drive north through Blyth, turn up a shady lane and park beside a meadow bounded by woods and farmers' fields. It is a peaceful place, a secret garden of wildflowers, with the woods on one side and a bank of trees separating it from the fields. Across from us near the edge of the meadow is a row of gravestones standing up like a tiny audience in a nearly deserted theatre. This is the old Anglican cemetery, the place where my mother and Gerry wish to be buried. No one has been buried here for a long time, perhaps a hundred years, and my mother does not know if it is possible, especially as she has never been a member of the Anglican Church, though Gerry grew up in it. She is investigating. She wants this very much. "It's like buying real estate," she says. "You really want to get in."

CHAPTER 7

Anne Laidlaw, Mother and Grandmother

DEATH OF ANNE LAIDLAW

In the winter of 1959, after a long and debilitating struggle with Parkinson's disease, Anne Laidlaw died in the Wingham hospital. Letters to my mother from her grandmother (Sadie), her sister Sheila, and her father describe Anne Laidlaw's precipitous decline and final disintegration, "the final break-up," as Robert put it. As early as 1957 my great-grandmother was writing to my mother: ". . . your mother is awfully thin and it's hard to describe how this disease is gradually breaking down her abilities. She has so little now to keep interested in. She can't read much and if her speech was good she could feel she was of use to answer phones for orders (for turkeys) or talk to friends."

Another letter Sadie wrote only weeks before Anne died, dated January 19, 1959, reminds me of the scene in "The Peace of Utrecht" (*Dance*) where the mother gets out of bed and runs away from the hospital. "It's hard to tell you Alice just how your mother really is, sometimes she is so confused one would think she was in a dream all the time and I understand from the nurse that she gets out of bed at night and out of her room, I suppose her dreams are so real to her she goes looking for Bob or thinks she is at home . . . she was here today and I made tea as soon as she came, we had nice McIntosh apple sauce and she ate two thin slices of Buttered Bread and the Cup of tea. It took her the hour to eat but of course she wanted to talk and I had to keep her at the eating. I suppose she was here an hour and a half she was getting real tired by the time Bob came at 4. Her speech is really bad but we got a word here and there and were able to understand the main idea, she talks so much and it seems as if her mind is in a turmoil and she has to talk to get relief, then too she longs for company but she does the talking and gets muddled . . ." The anguish, the volubility, and the neediness of the mother making an awful spectacle of herself in this nightmare scene are already familiar to me from stories.

My grandmother,
Anne Chamney,
at my parents' wedding in 1951.

There are no surprises here, only confirmation of what I already knew.

Ten days later, on January 29, 1959, she wrote with some urgency (in those days a long-distance phone call was a major undertaking) warning her granddaughter of the inevitable. "Daddy said this morning for me to write you and get it posted to go out today, your Mother Alice is slipping away, she has to have sedative to keep her quiet at night, We don't look for her to be here very long. . . . I feel so sorry for Bob he has done all he could to lighten her burden and has kept cheerful through it all. I feel badly for you so far away but it would be very foolish to come home in Winter time . . ."

My mother's sister Sheila (by that time married and living in Toronto, but still coming back to Wingham often) implored my mother not to even think of coming home at this time. It would be pointless. She mentioned how pitiful it was to see their mother in hospital disintegrating before their eyes. In the letter she is horrified that her grandmother and Aunt Maud are already talking about the clothes she should be buried in. (I think of the practicality of Aunt Annie and Auntie Lou in "The Peace of Utrecht," and of all the other Aunts in my mother's stories, and what they represent.)

I have in my possession a letter that Anne Laidlaw managed to write to my mother a few weeks before she died, the only letter of hers I have found. Undated, unsigned, and written in pencil, it reads:

Dearest dear,
I am just so full of love and good wishes that my letter will I fear it will burst at the corner. Please write soon (just for me) everything. I find my love and it is centred on my children.

Please write soon. At present I am in the hospital for a general check-up. I have very little done for Christmas but I suppose all will straighten itself out as it did in the past . . . So please write. My letter writing is terrible.

To me these words speak of a genuine spiritual breakthrough, not the emotional manipulations I was expecting to find. I find the letter heartbreaking, the attempt at normalcy in the face of catastrophe, the "check-up," the worries about Christmas presents, but most of all the last-ditch, all but incoherent declaration of love.

Of course she had gone into the hospital to die. My mother did not return to Ontario to see her when she was dying, nor did she attend the funeral. Travelling across the country by plane in those days meant long hours, bumpy flights, and frequent stopovers, and it was an expense my parents could scarcely afford. Our family visited Wingham (and Oakville) by car, in the summer of 1961, eighteen months after my grandmother's death. I was seven and Jenny was four.

On a dresser in one of the upstairs bedrooms in the house in Wingham I remember seeing a photograph of my grandmother in profile. She is pale with a high forehead and wiry hair springing up from her scalp. The photograph frightened me. It was as if she had died many, many years ago, in another era. In fact, I had seen my grandmother once, but I was much too young to remember her. My parents took me back east for the first time in the summer of 1954 when I was less than a year old. I'm told I screamed when she tried to hold me, I was so frightened. There is a photograph taken on that trip of the three Laidlaw siblings kneeling on the grass, my mother looking beautiful and sophisticated, crew-cut brother Bill, and sister Sheila in harlequin glasses. The three siblings went in totally different directions and something about the symmetry of this has always pleased me. Bill also went to Western but he took Sciences, and went on to attend Cal Tech before earning a Ph.D. in the fairly esoteric discipline of theoretical chemistry and becoming an academic, first in Edmonton, then Calgary. I remember flying to Edmonton with my mother for my Uncle Bill's wedding to Aunt Lucia in 1960, how loudly the engines droned all through that rocky flight in the dark and how I was afraid I was going to throw up. Sheila left Wingham as well, moving to Toronto to study at the Ontario College of Art.

An imperfect portrait of the Laidlaws from 1954. Back row (mostly headless): Sarah Code Laidlaw (my great-grandmother), Robert Laidlaw (my grandfather), Anne Laidlaw (my grandmother), my father, and me. Front row: my mother, Bill Laidlaw (my mother's brother), and Sheila Laidlaw (my mother's sister).

Within a few years she would be married and the mother of two boys. Standing in a row behind them are their parents and the older generation, but the photographer has aimed the camera too low so that all their heads have been cut off. I can see only my grandmother's hands held stiffly against her dress, like pieces of carved wood, curved and held together at the fingertips as if to keep them still.

FICTIONAL MOTHERS

The problem, the only problem, is my mother. And she is the one of course that I am trying to get; it is to reach her that this whole journey has been undertaken. With what purpose? To mark her off, to describe, to illuminate, to celebrate, to get rid of her; and it did not work, for she looms too close, just as she always did.

– "The Ottawa Valley," *Something I've Been Meaning to Tell You*

After our trip to Wingham and Oakville in 1961, my mother wrote "The Peace of Utrecht," the first of what she has called her "breakthrough stories." She had never been able to use personal material the way she does here. The idea for the story came from an incident that took place at her grandmother's house in Wingham. While she was visiting there, her grandmother took her upstairs and got out all her mother's clothes to see if she wanted them. The scene must have brought back all my mother's contradictory emotions over her mother's death.

In "The Peace of Utrecht," a young woman, Helen, returns home and visits with her sister Maddy after their mother has died. Underlying their laughter and surface camaraderie is a tension between them arising from the undeniable injustice of the situation. Maddy, "well over thirty," is the one who has stayed home to look after the sick mother for the past ten years while the narrator has gone away, gotten married, had a life, and has two children to show for it.

The sisters remember the horror of their mother's disintegration. "Our Gothic Mother, with the cold appalling mask of the Shaking Palsy laid across her features, shuffling, weeping, devouring attention wherever she can get it, eyes dead and burning, fixed inward on herself; this is not all," made even worse by the heartbreaking remissions, those days when it was as if the mother had awoken from a bad dream and was able to get out of bed, tidy up around the house, even bake a pie or do a little sewing.

They have dealt with their mother by becoming cold and matter-of-fact, withdrawing emotion from her "as you might take away meat from a prisoner to weaken him, till he died." Maddy says that towards the end, "She spent a lot of time sorting things. All kinds of things. Greeting cards. Buttons and yarn. Sorting and putting them into little piles. It would keep her quiet by the hour."

Through her old Aunt Annie, the narrator learns that Maddy had her mother put in hospital, telling her it was for a check-up, but really she put her there to die. The mother tried to escape from the hospital and after that a board was nailed across her bed. The story ends with Helen telling her sister, "Take your life," and Maddy replies, "But why can't I, Helen? *Why can't I?*"

When I read the more autobiographical stories, such as this one, I see my Aunt Sheila as Maddy (my aunt was not at all like Maddy), my mother as Helen, myself as the little girl Margaret, and my great-grandmother (Sadie) and my great-aunt Maud as the Aunts. In my mind the scenes take place in the brick farmhouse my mother grew up in and the house in town where my great-grandmother and great-aunt Maud lived, a house that did smell of polish and vinegar, at least I think it did – or am I only imagining that because I have read it in her story?

Reading is like dreaming; images flickering in our consciousness as our eyes move across the page. Usually these images come entirely from the imagination, we have to invent them, but when I read a story such as "The Peace of Utrecht," I cannot help putting people I know and places I've seen into my dreaming of the story. The effect is a heightened realism, like an Andrew Wyeth painting. Conversely, when I visit the places and people that gave rise to the stories, Wingham for instance, or the house where my mother grew up, they assume an added dimension for me, and I feel a rush of recognition, an intimacy, as if it's a movie set I'm visiting, and I know every single camera angle very well.

And I see my mother as the daughter in these stories: embarrassed, ashamed, horrified, guilty, but standing apart, not letting herself be overwhelmed by pity. Having to save herself, resisting something that was false and sentimental, resisting love because love means being engulfed.

The women relatives and the sick mother come up again in "Winter Wind" (*Something*). The narrator has to stay at her grandmother and Aunt Madge's house in town because of a blizzard. Their hallway is "polished, fragrant, smooth, cozy as the inside of a nutshell." Her grandmother is ironing, her Aunt Madge is making a carrot pie for dinner. All is lovely order and industry, and the girl is happy, at least until her grandmother inquires about home. "At supper my grandmother said, 'How is your mother?' and at once my spirits dropped. . . . 'I have a terrible time understanding her on the phone,' my grandmother said.

'It just seems the worse her voice gets, the more she wants to talk.'" The narrator reports that her mother has been painting the kitchen cupboards (the kind of thing Anne would do; she did actually paint a V for victory on the floor of the parlour to celebrate the end of the War), though "there was something crude and glaring" about the depictions of flowers and other objects with which she decorated each cupboard and door, "something that seemed to reflect the stiffness and intensity of the stage of the disease my mother had now got into," and the grandmother's disapproval is palpable: "She will be painting the cupboards when she would be better off getting your father's dinner."

The most purely autobiographical story about her mother was "The Ottawa Valley" (*Something*), which deals directly with her Parkinson's disease. Two sisters go with their mother by train to visit Aunt Dodie in the Ottawa Valley, where their mother grew up. Aunt Dodie sells milk for a living as her land is too poor to farm. They visit Dodie's sister-in-law, Aunt Lena, "stiff with terror," a backwoods girl who is expecting her ninth child, and Uncle James, with his lovely Irish accent and songs about drinking "the water of the barley."

The pivotal scene comes when the mother and daughter are about to go into church, and the elastic waistband on the girl's underpants snaps. The mother unfastens a safety pin that is holding her slip together at the shoulder and gives it to the daughter. When they are in church the mother's slip is drooping below her hemline and the daughter, impressed by the sacrifice, asks recklessly, "Is your arm going to stop shaking?" The mother doesn't answer. "For the first time she held out altogether against me."

In "Friend of My Youth," a woman describes her mother as

a young schoolteacher before she became ill, who taught in a one-room school in the Ottawa Valley (as Anne did), whose wedding dress is "to be appliquéd with silk roses, her veil held by a cap of seed pearls," just as Anne's dress and veil are in her wedding photo. The woman has a recurring dream in which her mother appears to her and has not died after all, in fact she has been quite well all these years, and the woman wonders how she could have forgotten how merry her mother was "before her throat muscles stiffened and a woeful, impersonal mask fastened itself over her features."

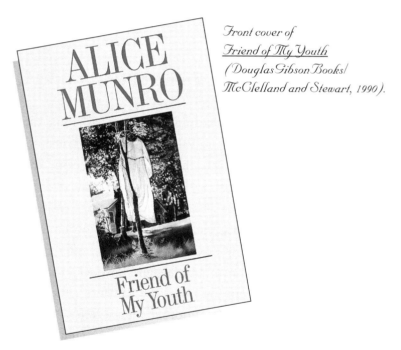

Front cover of
Friend of My Youth
(Douglas Gibson Books/
McClelland and Stewart, 1990).

When I try to imagine my grandmother, images float through my mind like the images in dreams; I see a figure calling out from the bed in a garbled voice; I see stiff fingers sorting buttons or pinning up a hem of a dress she is making for her daughter. I see her as a composite of Del's mother Ada in *Lives of Girls and Women*, the mother who runs away from the hospital in "The Peace of Utrecht," the mother whose arm won't stop shaking in "The Ottawa Valley," the mother who rises from her sickbed to paint flowers on the kitchen cupboards in "Winter Wind," the light-hearted young teacher planning her wedding in "Friend of My Youth." My grandmother was someone I never knew in person, but I feel I know far more about her, even things my mother might not know, through these fictional recreations and what I read into them, than most of us can ever hope to know about a grandmother.

THE CHAMNEYS IN THE OTTAWA VALLEY

Anne Clarke Chamney came from a family of Irish Protestants who arrived in the Ottawa Valley from County Wicklow in 1820, at about the same time that the Laidlaws came from Scotland to Toronto. They settled at a place called Scotch Corners, near Carleton Place in Lanark County. Apparently they were enticed to come to Canada because of a movement to settle sturdy Protestants in the Ottawa Valley as a buffer against Catholic Quebec to the north. But the land was rockier and the soil thinner than it was in the places the Laidlaws settled, and the family was very poor. My mother's grandfather, George Chamney, married Bertha Stanley, a schoolteacher who became intensely religious in later life. (In *Lives of Girls and Women*, Ada tells Del the story of her mother coming into a little money and spending it all on bibles, even though the family was so desperately poor.) The story "The Progress of Love" is based on what my mother knew about Bertha's life.

Bertha's father was a maker of sleighs and sleds, and her mother was Catherine Clarke, whose ring my mother wears, and whose embroidery sampler hangs in her kitchen in Clinton. The sampler depicts a house with rows of windows and a chimney like a child's drawing, with the words "Catherine Clarke" and the date, 1837, embroidered beneath it. When she was growing up, my mother heard stories about Catherine Clarke, who was something of a heroine in the family. It was hinted that her husband was a womanizer and that Catherine was terribly unhappy. She died fairly young, after a nervous breakdown, and it is possible her death was a suicide. In doing some research, my mother discovered that she falsified her age on a census (she was older than her husband) and switched from Anglicanism to Presbyterianism in an age when it was very unusual for a woman not to belong to the same church as her Anglican husband.

George and Bertha's daughter Anne was born in 1897. She ran away from the farm, where it was expected that she would continue to help out, to go to school. My mother thought she was "incredibly brave" to do this. She borrowed money from a schoolteacher cousin of hers, and enrolled in Normal School (the teachers' training institution of the day) at Carleton Place. The first year she came down with scarlet fever and dropped out, but she borrowed money again, and returned to get her teaching certificate. She headed out west on her own and taught in Alberta at a place called Killem, east of Edmonton (Alberta had only become a province in 1904), one of four teachers in a consolidated school. For her the time on the Prairies was a happy, lighthearted adventure; she told my mother about the practical jokes the teachers played on each other, the shenanigans they got up to. Later she returned to the

Ottawa Valley, and advanced to the position of principal of a four-room school, which was as far as a woman teacher could go in those days. Then, of course, she met Robert Laidlaw at Blyth, quit teaching, and began her married life in Wingham.

MARRIED LIFE

The wedding photograph reveals a pretty young woman (my mother said she was lovely, with classic Irish looks: dark blue eyes, and a beautiful pink and white complexion) looking confident and composed, wearing a veil across her forehead in the twenties style and a diaphanous dress with appliquéd flowers and leaves on it, white gloves in hand and a bouquet. Robert, standing behind her, looks surprisingly handsome, with one eyebrow raised quizzically. The couple settled down at their new

*My mother's parents,
Robert Laidlaw and
Anne Chamney,
on their wedding day in 1927.*

home outside of Wingham. Anne had saved enough money from teaching for them to purchase a nine-acre parcel of land bordering on the Maitland River just west of town.

As for the attraction her parents felt for each other, my mother speaks of the widespread antipathy so many women had towards men and the male life at that time, "the free-wheeling, drinking, swearing, dangerous male life." Robert Laidlaw would have appealed to Anne because he was not like so many other men. He was a good man and someone she felt she could control. She had been engaged twice before, and may have broken off the engagements because her suitors failed to meet her rigorous standards. When she married him, she made Robert promise that he would never drink alcohol for the rest of his life, and he never did, at least not while she was alive. (I do remember drinking his sweet, homemade dandelion wine from juice glasses in my later visits to Wingham.) My mother wonders if they were ever in love. She could never tell, because there was so little communication or spontaneous affection between them; after marriage a "stiff masquerade came down over them."

When she was growing up, the relationship between her parents was a mystery to my mother. They lived totally separate, parallel lives, both full of work. They were never demonstrative. All signs of affection between them were muted. They called each other Mother and Father, or at least Anne called Robert "Daddy" or "Dad," and Robert called Anne "Mother." Like most children of any age, the thought of her parents having sex filled her with revulsion. When she told me this she asked me, "Can you imagine it? Can you imagine your parents having sex?" She hated the way her mother's breasts hung down "like pan-cakes," and she shuddered at the "terrible flesh-coloured undergarments done up with hooks and eyes." And it wasn't such a sanitized world then. Bodies smelled. In the world she knew "people only had a bath once a week so there was always a definite smell of flesh, underclothes and bedclothes, not a bad smell but a human smell."

This revulsion toward the flesh, particularly the flesh of the parents, is explored in "Miles City, Montana" (*Progress*), when, at the funeral of a boy who has drowned, the narrator remembers how she felt as a young girl about the bodies of the adults around her. "Children sometimes have an access of disgust concerning adults. The size, the lumpy shapes, the bloated power. The breath, the coarseness, the hairiness, the horrid secretions." The disgust goes beyond this; it has to do with the mortality of their flesh, and the flesh of the children they have brought into the world. "They gave consent to the death of children and to my death not by anything they said or thought but by the very fact that they had made children – they had made me."

MOTHER AND DAUGHTER

On July 10, 1931, when she was thirty-four years old, after two miscarriages, Anne gave birth to a daughter, Alice Ann, who would be followed by a son, William, in 1936, after another miscarriage, and a daughter, Sheila, in 1937. There is a photograph of Anne outside the house in Wingham cradling beautiful baby Alice securely bundled in knitted clothes and bonnet. You can't see the mother's face very well, as she is looking down at the baby. She is a large-boned woman with strong features, dressed up in a wool suit, heels, stockings, and a hat with a turned-up brim.

My mother with her mother, in the yard at Wingham in 1931.

In those early years before her brother and sister were born, Alice was an adored and prized child, turned out in fine clothes painstakingly sewn by hand (Anne was an ambitious and creative seamstress, like the mother in "Red Dress – 1946" who sews a red velvet dress for her daughter to wear to a high-school dance), and her hair was set in ringlets with a wet comb every morning (a procedure my mother hated). The rosebud mouth, full cheeks and bouncing ringlets gave her a Mary Pickford charm, the embodiment of all the ideas of gentility and culture to which Anne aspired. Early on, Anne made much of her daughter's phenomenal memory and precocity. By the time she was three or four, Alice was reciting poetry on a live radio program in Wingham, *The Kiddies' Half Hour*. At first she enjoyed showing off, effortlessly reeling off mostly comic recitations. (Recitation was a dying form of entertainment when she was a girl, all but unknown by the time she was in high school. It was the end of an age of a kind of hometown theatre.) As she got older she saw that this type of behaviour did not make you popular in a place like Wingham, where "people might see you as a freak or a genius, depending on their perspective." Where they might ask, who do you think you are?

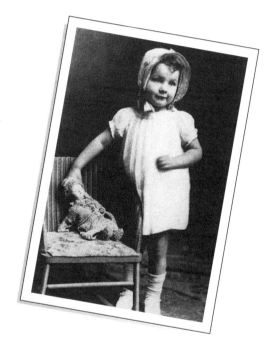

My mother at around three years old.

From the beginning the relationship between mother and daughter was difficult. Young Alice felt she had to resist her mother's control over her. As an educated woman who considered herself a modern mother, Anne subscribed to contemporary child-raising ideas about keeping bodily functions to a rigid schedule. Eating, sleeping, and bowel movements all had to be on a timetable, regardless of the needs of the child. In the name of these "progressive" ideas, she even administered enemas to her daughter, a practice which embedded in my mother a deep and lasting sense of humiliation.

My mother told me Anne's interference in her daughter's life was highly unusual for that time and place. Most other women in the farming communities of rural Ontario had neither the time nor the inclination to meddle in their children's lives to nearly the extent that she did. They usually weren't educated, they didn't have middle-class aspirations, and they usually had more children than her mother did, so that between washing, ironing, scrubbing, and cooking, there wasn't much time for worrying about how the children would turn out. "It was enough to keep them clean with clothes on their backs. Maintaining cleanliness and respectability was a huge job for most women."

As she got older, young Alice felt constantly that she was being judged as bad, that she was always in conflict with her

My mother with her dog, Major, in front of the house at Wingham.

mother. At least once a month, she got into serious trouble of some kind. And it wasn't just with her mother. "I didn't know an adult who wasn't critical of me all the time." At school she was getting in trouble for being "inept, stupid, and terribly messy." Her handwriting was so bad that one teacher called her "Uncle Wiggly." Remember how Del is shaking so badly she starts the treadle sewing machine accidentally and is exempted from sewing? That was my mother. Of course neatness and skill at needlework were more important in a girl than almost anything else in those days, though the letters from my great-grandmother do refer to my mother's triumphs at school, so it couldn't have been all bad.

At home she kept getting in trouble for those things and for everything else, for being sarcastic, for being nasty. "I always talked back. I wasn't a nice child, at that time lots of girls were nice, but being nice meant such a terrible abdication of self." (I don't want her to say this. Surely she *was* nice. I was nice. I wanted to please her. Did I abdicate *my* self?) Her earliest strategy in life was one of protecting herself, thinking her survival depended on it. She often lied and hoped not to be found out, though of course lying was considered a terrible sin.

At the time when Anne was starting to get sick, overtaken by mysterious attacks of lethargy, but before she had any inkling that she was in the early stages of Parkinson's disease, she and her daughter had terrible rows, which culminated in my mother being beaten by her father, in much the same way Rose is punished in "Royal Beatings" in *Who Do You Think You Are?* The arguments between mother and daughter would escalate. My mother would refuse to back down, daring to "talk back" rather than capitulate. Finally her father would be called in from the barn, and Anne would tell her version of events. What my mother found most painful was her perception that "a story was being told on me that wasn't true" and that she was never allowed to tell her side of the story. When things got really bad, which happened two or three times a year, her father would go get his leather belt and beat her with it, exactly the way Rose's father does after Flo calls him in from the barn when she has had enough of Rose's flippancy. "'All right,' says Flo. 'You've done it this time. All right.' . . . Rose tries to butt in, to say it isn't true." But by then it is too late. She could not write that story, another of her "breakthrough" stories, until after her father had died.

I was surprised when my mother told me about how very puritanical her family life was, and how puritanical she was herself; surprised because that isn't how I have ever seen my mother, and that is not at all what it was like in our household when I was growing up. In her home, any mention of sex was taboo, of course, and so was swearing. Alcohol was "a badge of sin." When my mother saw a bottle of whisky sitting on the kitchen counter in someone's house, she was shocked. Anyone who drank was a "scoundrel" and a "wastrel."

She was also quite a "churchmouse" who attended the Anglican Church with a friend, and found it aesthetically much more appealing than her own United Church (as Del does in *Lives*). She lost her faith when she was about twelve; every time she asked for a "sign" from God and no sign was forthcoming her faith "went down a notch." It didn't matter much because at about this time "art took over." Art became her religion.

According to my mother, Anne "was a very controlling person but her control was not just a personal control, it was the control of a moral order she believed in and projected on to others. She was full of self-assertion; she had no self-doubt and naturally she would clash with a daughter who questioned everything, who resisted any form of control." Anne's values were based on a model of gentility that came from the Victorian period. My mother considers that rural, small-town Ontario was essentially Victorian up until the Second World War, and that she grew up in the last remnants of that age.

Like Ada in *Lives of Girls and Women,* Anne believed that the only way a woman could have her own life, her own autonomy, was to reject sex completely. Giving in to desire meant sacrificing your self and all your prospects. As an educated woman of her time, she was an old-style feminist who stood for purity and the temperance league, and my mother has often referred to her mother's violent, almost pathological hatred of sex. There is something of the primness and prudery of that earlier brand of feminism (where women had to be pure and virtuous) underpinning Ada's famous speech to her daughter in *Lives of Girls and Women.* "There is a change coming I think in the lives of girls and women. Yes. But it is up to us to make it come. All women have had up to now is their connection with men. . . . Don't be distracted. Once you make that mistake of being distracted over a man, your life will never be your own." If you truly wanted to own your life, you had to be pure, you had to become an Albanian virgin.

Of course Del does not follow this advice. "Del felt it was not so different from all the other advice handed out to women, to girls, advice that assumed being female made you damageable, that a certain amount of carefulness and solemn fuss and self-protection were called for, whereas men were supposed to be able to go out and take on all kinds of experience and shuck off what they didn't want and come back proud. Without even thinking about it, I had decided to do the same."

Del does get herself distracted over Garnet French, and she does come close to losing herself until the pivotal moment in the baptism scene when Garnet has been holding her head under water and she finally comes up for air and everything has changed; she realizes it has all been a game. Del wakes up in time and is lucky enough not to have gotten pregnant. Ultimately I don't think she regrets her involvement with him. What is most important to her is the freedom to have the experience the way men have always had. It's a new kind of feminism.

In the character of Ada my mother has emphasized the strong, unconventional, practical side of her mother, while downplaying the pathetic, half-crazed, sick side. Ada is more like the mother of a friend she knew in West Vancouver than her own mother. Ada comes across as self-possessed and independent, with a thirst for knowledge and culture: she listens to the opera, she joins a book-discussion group, she moves into town. She is more the victim of circumstances than anything else, trapped within the narrowness of small-town society and disapproving aunts. Illness is barely hinted at, described only as a falling-off of energy. And she has an innocent lack of awareness about how others see her, and Del sees how this makes her vulnerable – although, of course, being oblivious can be a strength as well.

GENTEEL ASPIRATIONS

In the years of poverty and hardship following her marriage, Anne cared very much about creating some standard of gentility and beauty in her surroundings. This was terribly difficult, given the family's financial situation, but she did manage to acquire some lovely things for her home, which my mother remembers.

"Poor Mother. She was so creative but she had no money. We had some beautiful furniture in our house which no one appreciated. She afforded it by bartering, she bartered fox furs, and we had the most beautiful dining-room suite that I'd ever seen, it wasn't comfortable but it was exquisite. . . . She bought these goblets that I still have, pressed glass goblets, beautiful things. She said to me once after she had been sick for a long time that she would lie there in bed imagining houses and how she would furnish them. I do the same thing now. Her individual stamp on things wasn't appreciated by anyone, not me, not my father, not my grandmother appreciated what she was doing – which didn't really disturb her. I think she really believed in it. As she got sicker and sicker her grasp got fainter. Oh God I can hardly bear, Sheila, to think about her life. It's so awful because she didn't have anybody . . ."

Essentially Anne was a conventional person, not an intellectual or a rebel. What she really wanted was to have the kind of life "where she could have ladies over for tea." My mother is convinced that if she had lived long enough to see them in print, she would never have approved of the stories her daughter wrote; she would have been horrified by the sex in them. And she wouldn't have wanted the life of an artist for her daughter. She would have wanted her to be a genteel lady writer like L.M. Montgomery, preferably married to a doctor or a lawyer.

My mother thinks it would have been better for her mother to have kept on teaching, that she needed another outlet for her energies, but at that time there was no choice once a woman was married. By the time it was possible for a married woman to teach, when there was a shortage of male teachers after the War began, she was too sick to work.

Unlike the Laidlaws, who set themselves apart from the world, an alien land seen from a great distance, who viewed with suspicion people who could go out and do things, Anne felt at home in the world and was not ashamed to take advantage of what the world had to offer. She had a good business sense, a trait that was not very evident on the Laidlaw side of the family (or at least in that branch of the family; other Laidlaw relatives became the wealthy owners of the Laidlaw trucking firm, now an international concern). In different circumstances my mother imagines Anne could have become an antiques dealer.

In her poignant essay "Working for a Living," my mother describes how Anne made a trip up to the Muskoka resort area in the summer of 1940 to sell fox furs to American tourists, thereby saving the family from financial ruin. In this role, she saw her mother as a brave and enterprising woman, with "the true instinct, for mixing friendship and business considerations, that all good salespeople have." She remembers how she and her father came to fetch her mother after the fur-selling venture, which had turned out to be a success. For a moment the daughter doesn't recognize the woman in the hotel lobby, who is "brisk and elegant, her dark hair parted in the middle and pinned up in a neat coronet of braids. She had crossed effortlessly into the world of the hotel."

As the years went by, Anne's pretensions to a genteel, middle-class existence became more and more unrealistic. When my mother was in high school, Anne set up a scholarship fund after an uncharacteristically good year in the fox-farming business. The Laidlaw Fox-Fur Scholarship for the amount of twenty-five dollars was to be awarded by the school each year to the student attaining the highest marks in the entrance exams. Through the hard years that followed, when the money represented a huge amount of the family income that was desperately needed at home, Anne persisted in offering the scholarship out of pride, out of a belief that times would soon get better. To my mother a gesture of such largesse in the midst of real poverty seemed almost perverse.

THE SHAKING PALSY

When Anne was in her mid-forties (and my mother about ten), she began experiencing a range of disturbing symptoms. Like the mother in "The Ottawa Valley" (*Something*), her arm wouldn't stop shaking. "Just her left forearm trembled. The hand trembled more than the arm. The thumb knocked ceaselessly against the palm." Her voice was becoming unintelligible, and my mother had to act as translator. As time went on she became less and less capable of sewing or doing the housework, which became her older daughter's responsibility.

Finally, when my mother was about fourteen, Anne went down to London to see a specialist, who diagnosed Parkinson's disease. My mother described how she came back to Wingham hard hit by the diagnosis. "She knew it was hopeless. . . . She could no longer walk or eat or talk normally, she was stiffening out of control. There was no cure, no medication she could take." At least the disease was not hereditary, and she was quick to reassure her children of that fact.

Anne contracted Parkinson's disease as a direct result of having had a viral infection known as the sleeping sickness (encephalitis lethargica) when she was a young teacher in the

Ottawa Valley. The "sleepy sickness," as it was called, followed on the heels of the more famous "Spanish Flu" pandemic of the winter of 1918–19, alluded to in "Carried Away" (*Open Secrets*), when the librarian keeps the library open even though the flu is rampaging through the town. Appearing first in Austria, sleeping sickness, a lesser-known but equally virulent virus, was to spread over the globe over a ten-year period, killing five million people and disabling millions more. Anne came down with the disease in 1924 or 1925, and apparently hers was a relatively mild case. She knew something was wrong when she was teaching a class and suddenly she wasn't able to write on the blackboard because her hand was shaking.

Encephalitis lethargica was a particularly bizarre affliction. Some patients were unable to sleep at all (the sleep centre of the brain had been destroyed), while others had the opposite reaction and fell into a sleep that lasted weeks. About a third of those afflicted with the virus died during the course of the infection; some died after weeks of sleeplessness, while others lapsed into comas from which they never awoke. Of those who survived, the majority later contracted a bizarre form of Parkinson's disease called post-encephalitic syndrome, ten, fifteen, or twenty years after the original infection. By the nineteen-sixties, asylums all over the world were full of these forgotten post-encephalitic cases. The hallmarks of Parkinson's disease – tremor (the disease was originally called "the Shaking Palsy") and an increasing rigidity of the body – were present in post-encephalitic patients. But, according to writer and physician Oliver Sacks, this was no " 'ordinary' Parkinson's disease, but a disorder of far greater complexity, severity and strangeness."

Sacks is the author of the extraordinary book *Awakenings*, a record of the lives of post-encephalitic patients before and after they were given the L-dopa drug in 1969, the so-called miracle drug that "awakened" these patients as if from the dead. He described patients who were like living corpses, immobilized for months or even years at a time in a trance-like state, others who couldn't stop repeating a movement, still others who became frozen in a position for hours before being able to break out of it, and he speculated that these patients were struggling with "disorders of movement and push." When they wanted to move, a counterforce would come in to block the move. Or when they wanted to stop a movement, they were unable to do so. The part of the brain that initiated and regulated movement had been damaged and these patients were trapped in the torment of a futile inner struggle.

When these patients were given massive doses of L-dopa, which replenished the supply of dopamine in the brain, they went through a series of extraordinary transformations, or "awakenings," as he called them. People who had been virtually unable to move for years on end came out of their trance, got up out of their wheelchair, walked, and spoke, with no impairment whatsoever. Then they usually relapsed into their former state.

I wonder if Anne Laidlaw's bizarre behaviour was a result of these specific problems and not just the way she coped with her disease; in other words, I wonder if the behaviours (the hurrying, the restlessness, the endless talking – "Your mother wanted to talk") were a physical manifestation of the disease itself, rather than the result of how her particular character dealt with her disease.

Anne was to live another fifteen years with the sometimes intermittent but always inexorable progress of the disease. My mother thinks that for someone like her the illness was particularly tragic because she had the kind of extroverted temperament that demanded engagement with the world. She did not have much of an inner life to sustain her. She would complain to visitors, to anyone who would listen, really, about how everything had been taken from her: her voice, the ability to make things with her hands, any possibility of a social life.

My mother's childhood home at Wingham in the 1930s.

As a teenager, my mother resented the unceasing demands for comfort and solicitude, the calls for visits and cups of tea, for cheerful conversation. My mother did what she had to, but she resisted the role of the dutiful daughter, preferring instead to assert her own individuality and contrariness. "We argued. She would rally her strength and struggle with me, long after she had given up on ordinary work and appearances." It is understandable to me that young Alice shut herself off emotionally from her mother's illness, with its particularly isolating and grotesque symptoms, because she feared that she would not be able to bear the waves of pity and grief that would engulf her. Maybe arguing was a more authentic means of communication, a way of cutting through the sentimental excesses of "poor Mother."

My mother escaped from home temporarily when she won the scholarship to go to university, and permanently when she married my father and moved to Vancouver two years later, putting all this geographical distance between them, but she never really got away from Anne. To this day she is deeply affected by the isolation and suffering of her mother's life, and tormented by the way she closed herself off from her. Over lunch at The Old House Restaurant in Courtenay she told me about her mother's illness, how her hands were shaky, her voice garbled, how she was ashamed to bring any of her friends home. "Oh, Sheila," she said, "she had no . . . one," and my mother began to sob, but her sobs were muffled by the clatter of cutlery and the hum of conversation around us.

CHAPTER 8

The Making of a Writer
1931–1949

THE EDGE OF TOWN

If you walk out from town along this westward road, you pass the grey wooden houses where old people live; they live in the back kitchens and leave the front rooms empty. Then you pass the boarded-up glove factory, and a junkyard where the wrecked cars lie overturned, rusting in thistles. Beyond this is a tamarack tree and a narrow iron bridge over the creek; the tree was struck by lightning once, and did not die, but grew crooked afterwards – all the upper branches reach out to one side. The tall, misshapen tree is like a sign saying: Here is an end, here is a difference. And here is an end, the end of town. The sidewalk does not go any further, there are no more street lamps, and the town policeman does not cross the bridge.
– "The Edge of Town," Queen's Quarterly, 1955

The stories my mother told about her childhood back east made her life seem inconceivably harsh and full of extremes. Even the weather was unimaginable. She told us about walking in a blizzard to get to school and how one winter (the winter of 1935) it was so cold many of the trees actually died, and she could hear them cracking and groaning in their death throes. She told us about life on the farm, about old horses being slaughtered to provide food for the foxes and mink, about kittens born in the barn being drowned. She told us about the mink panicking and eating their own young when the planes from the Port Albert air base droned overhead during the War, and about putting baby mink in the stove once to keep them warm. She described the humiliation of bringing her friends home and having to act as translator because her mother's voice was so garbled from Parkinson's disease she could not be understood.

The geographical and psychological landscape of my mother's childhood world was about as different from my own as was possible to imagine. While I grew up on the edge of the dripping rainforest in the shadow of a mountain with the ocean freighters visible from our front windows in the young port city of Vancouver, she looked out upon cultivated fields, gently rolling hills, and nineteenth-century brick farmhouses. Where I experienced the constant drizzle of rain and a permeating dampness, with occasional outbursts of merciful sunshine, she lived through seasonal extremes, through blizzards and snow-drifts nestled "like sleeping whales" around her house, through floods and droughts, and plagues of mosquitoes of almost Biblical proportions. In our West Coast house we had the middle-class amenities, the wringer washer, a modern fridge and stove, while in her home there was an ice box, a wood-burning stove, and no running water or indoor plumbing until she was at least ten years old.

A writer friend of my mother's admitted to her that she wished she'd had the kind of deprived background my mother had had instead of her own middle-class upbringing, so that she would have the kind of material my mother had to draw on. I have the same feeling that my mother's experience was more vivid, more dramatic, more real than mine could ever be, because as a child she was exposed to poverty, to brutality, to illness from which there was no recovery, to a world which was fallen. There was no turning away for her. There was no fence around her yard. For her the only escape was through the imagination.

The house at the end of the Lowertown Road was an outpost of civility, a bastion of genteel aspirations, where books were read, where opera was listened to on the radio, where knowledge and education were held in the highest regard. To the east was Wingham, a town of about two thousand inhabitants – typical of dozens of towns in the farming country of Huron County – whose church spires she could just see when there were no leaves on the trees. Between her house and Wingham lay Lowertown itself, that no-man's-land beyond the "edge of town," where the civilizing influences of town petered out, where the policeman did not go. The fact that Lowertown had to be crossed before getting into town, and the conventional, narrow, safe world that town represented, where her grandmother, her Aunt Maud, and all the Aunts in her fiction lived, was hugely significant. She was an outsider. The town was a world she was not part of, a place she could only look at from a distance. It was significant to her as well that when she looked to the west what she saw were fields and woods, and not a single dwelling or building, which was quite unusual in that part of the country. It was view that delighted her because it symbolized something still wild and untamed.

In so much of my mother's fiction there is some lurking danger, like the man swinging his axe as he walks through the woods in "Images" – "you discover what you fear is nothing but the truth." Or there is a narrow escape, like the dark shape of a car without its lights on that narrowly misses the family in "Labor Day Dinner," or the near-drowning of the daughter in "Miles City, Montana." In her childhood she could not avoid seeing that death was real. How else is she able to take her readers to the brink of the unthinkable – a daughter having to assist her father perform abortions in "Before the Change" (*Love*), a gruesome murder-suicide in "Fits" (*Progress*), the hatred of a dying woman in "The Love of a Good Woman" – and back again? Is it easier to face the truth and to investigate, to explore, when you have never had the luxury of turning away from it?

DRIVING TO WINGHAM – JULY 1998

Today we are driving to Wingham, about twenty miles north of Clinton. We approach the town from the south and I see the shallow expanse of the Maitland River to the west and the church spires up ahead almost hidden by trees. Then we are on the main street and Gerry points out the town hall, an imposing brick building with high arched windows. "That's where your mother had the epiphany," he says in that way he has of being both serious and ironic at the same time. In those days the library was in the town hall (like the library Naomi and Del visit in *Lives of Girls and Women*, where Del digs up a graphic description of childbirth in a novel for her less literary friend to read). "Yes, that was where you saw the horses in the snow, wasn't it?" I ask her, feeling a bit like a journalist conducting an interview, taking in the sights of Alice Munro country.

"Yes it was."

In the introduction to the paperback edition of the *Selected Stories*, my mother described an experience she had while staring out those windows. She had checked out her books and she was watching the falling snow, when she saw a team of horses pulling a sleigh, moving onto the town weigh-scales. She was fifteen years old.

> *The sleigh was piled high with sacks of grain. The man who was driving the team had a winter cap pulled down on his head, fur-lined flaps over his ears. . . . This description makes the scene seem as if it was waiting to be painted and hung on the wall to be admired by somebody who has probably never bagged grain. The patient horses with their nobly rounded rumps, the humped figure of the driver, the coarse fabric of the sacks. The snow conferring dignity and peace. I didn't see it framed and removed in that way. I saw it alive and potent, and it gave me something like a blow to the chest. What does this mean, what can be discovered about it, what is the rest of the story? The man and the horses are not symbolic or picturesque, they are moving through a story which is hidden, and now, for a moment, carelessly revealed.*

We drive by the house where my great-grandmother and Great-Aunt Maud lived, cross the river and turn onto the Lowertown Road. Just across the bridge is a grassy meadow, the site of notorious Lowertown School, a brutal environment like the school in "Privilege" (*Who?*), with its filthy toilets and scenes of degradation, where Rose falls in love with Cora, who paints her fingernails. This is where my mother skipped a grade because she was the only student who passed grade one; the school she endured for two years before her mother insisted on switching her to the school in town, as Ada does with Del in *Lives of Girls and Women.*

Lowertown Road (the very word Lowertown speaks for itself) appears to be an innocuous stretch of road on the outskirts of town flanked by tidy homes on small acreages, and fields stretching beyond. Yet for me there is a heightened, cinematic dimension which is difficult to reconcile with what I'm seeing, because of course I'm imagining the notorious Flats Road from *Lives.* I'm thinking of bootleggers, criminals, and boys yelling out obscenities, of freaks like the swaggering dwarf, Becky Tyde, from "Royal Beatings" (*Who?*) or Stump Troy from "Executioners" (*Something*). I think of danger and evil, houses set on fire, murders.

We come to a crossroads and the Lowertown Road ends abruptly. To the right is the old Cruickshank property, and to the left the house my mother grew up in. We turn down the lane, past the field where the turkey barn used to be, and park in front of the house itself. It's a yellow-brick house, with a pattern of lighter bricks where the walls are joined together, gabled windows upstairs, and a side entrance to the porch and the kitchen, the part of the house that was the original homestead. As a child I thought it was quite a grand house, though not as grand as my other grandparents' house in Oakville, but it did have an upstairs, and gables, which I associated with mansions. Now there are car wrecks scattered across the yard and a sign on the front door saying Beauty Salon, Esthetician's Studio, Hair Waxing, Manicures. The whole place has an air of cheerful dereliction.

When we visited my grandfather on our trips back east, we

did not use that door, we entered the house by the back door through an enclosed porch that led into the kitchen. Off the kitchen was an alcove, which was like a bachelor's quarters, where my grandfather would lie on an old couch reading. From the kitchen I could see the back of his bald head and the book propped up in front of him. The porch and kitchen and alcove were the original homestead. I believe my grandfather lived almost entirely in this part of the house, and that he slept in the alcove, too. I thought he slept there because the main house reminded him of all the years his wife was bedridden with Parkinson's disease. I wondered about this arrangement when he married Etta, and thought it likely he wouldn't have shared a bed with her.

The Wingham house in 1990.

"MORE THAN AN ESCAPE"

"You have to start [writing] early and you have to want it more than just about anything else."
— from an interview with Graeme Gibson

I used to believe that my mother's talent, or genius or whatever you wish to call it, had sprung forth of its own accord, like Venus on the half shell, without much effort or work on her part. To some extent this was true; storytelling came to her so naturally and so early that she was "dazzled" by what she could produce at fifteen or sixteen. Now, of course, I know that after a period of youthful excitement she did undergo a long and arduous apprenticeship, beginning stories and novels then having to abandon them, suffering long periods of writer's block, getting depressed by rejections. By the time she was writing the kind of stories she wanted to write she was in her early thirties, and she had been writing for about twenty years.

Before she ever got the idea of being a writer, my mother imagined that she would be famous. She tells of riding to the slaughterhouse with her father to get the leftover tripe to feed the foxes and mink, and pretending that the grass in the fields was a crowd waving to her. She got the idea from a book about Queen Elizabeth I and her coronation.

When she was very young she led a very solitary life. She was the oldest child, and for the first five years of her life the only child, before the birth of her brother Bill and sister Sheila. She didn't have a chance to mix with other children or learn to do the things they did. "I didn't play with other children because I didn't live in town. I didn't know how to roller skate or ride a

My mother on her first day of school.

tricycle. I didn't know anything about skipping or playing with a ball. At Lowertown School we didn't do such things."

Even after starting at the town school in grade four, she characterized herself as "less skilled than everybody else, awkward and shy, the youngest in my class, and in a constant state of humiliation." Hence the teacher's joke about her "Uncle Wiggly" handwriting. I imagine her being like the girl in "Red Dress – 1946" who lives in terror of being asked to do a math problem at the blackboard, or being called on to answer a question in class. She suffered from an extreme self-consciousness and an exaggerated fear of being mocked. "Probably people didn't mock me that much because I was normal looking, but still I was an odd person."

My mother did not know how to get over these fears, but she found a way of displacing them. To split herself off from the miseries and humiliations of her day-to-day existence she began to live as much as possible in an imaginary world of stories and fantasies that coexisted with the real world of her experience. To her delight, she found this parallel imaginary world enormously satisfying, the answer to how to live her life. "It was more than an escape; it was a solution. It was better than being popular and knowing how to skip. It started as a redemption but pretty soon the art became more than a redemption, it was a wonderful experience. It wasn't just as if it was in the future, I was living it now, the whole movie thing, the whole involvement in this glamorous world."

When she was about eight years old she began to fantasize about being a movie star and how her life would be: "I had found a movie magazine in the bottom of a closet of someone's house where I was visiting and it had a picture of Deanna Durbin's wedding. Deanna Durbin was a movie star of the time and a singer. She was married in 1939 and she had about twenty bridesmaids." She transferred all the details about the wedding into her own fantasies.

When she got a little older she shifted her imagination over to the movies she would star in, and even thought about writing those movies herself: "It veered off fairly early from the clothes and the quintuplets to the kind of movies I would star in. I never got to see any movies because my mother didn't approve of me going to movies, the kinds of movies whose titles appealed to me. I would look at the stills outside the Lyceum Theatre. I wanted to be in *Gone with the Wind*. That was the beginning of making up stories, and then pretty soon I thought that I would write the movies and then star in them. This was when I was eight or nine years old. I had all this time to do it because I was not popular and I did not have friends."

I don't know if my mother would have become a writer if she hadn't grown up in an isolated environment; her childhood is a textbook case for the argument that social deprivation, coupled with access to books, can create a climate in which the artist's imagination flourishes. If she had seen *Gone with the Wind* and not just the stills, if she had found lots of movie magazines to look at and not just the one treasure she discovered in a closet, if she had had friends, would she have been as compelled to make up stories? Unanswerable questions. By the time she was eleven or twelve she was not quite so unpopular any more; she had arrived at "some lower level of popularity and acceptability," but now it didn't matter so much because by that time she was writing seriously.

By the age nine or ten she was composing verses while she was doing the housework. They were conventional nature poems, quatrains or rhyming couplets in iambic pentameter about the seasons, with occasional forays into blank verse, all of which she wrote down in a notebook that has not survived. Before long, she conceived an idea for a novel that she was working out in her head, constructing a parallel imaginary world that could be superimposed over the daily round of activities and chores.

"I was about eleven and I was planning a big historical novel. What I was writing was poetry; that I did write down. But the novel was going to be about the history of Huron County, from my Aunt Maud's life, and I did a lot in my head about what would happen and what the scenery would be like, what the feeling would be like. I was doing it [writing it in her head] in grade seven. I would do it on the long walks home from school or when I was doing housework, like making beds or doing dishes."

When she was a little older she got a new idea for a novel, about a woman whose lover is killed during the War. Here again, she did not write anything down; it was enough to imagine the story.

Then when she was fourteen she read *Wuthering Heights*, which came into her hands through the Book of the Month Club her mother belonged to for one year. It was part of a set that went with *Jane Eyre*, the 1943 Random House edition illustrated with the marvellous wood engravings by Fritz Eichenberg. Her mother tried to hide it from her; apparently, even the tame *Jane Eyre* had a very bad reputation. *Wuthering Heights* had an enormous impact on her; it was the book that changed her life more than any other. For months she lived and breathed that novel, and was reading it more or less all the time. Now she began working out a "Wuthering Heightsey" type novel she called "Charlotte Muir," which kept her going all through high school. She wrote the scenes and worked out the action in her head, afraid that if she wrote down an inferior version she would lose the magic of the story.

Charlotte Muir is the beautiful heroine with dark red hair, dark eyes, and white skin who is living alone on an isolated farm up in the hills after her parents have died. She has supernatural powers but doesn't know yet exactly what those powers are. (Was my mother writing unconsciously about her own future writing powers?) Charlotte wanders aimlessly over the moors making circles of stones, and longs to get away. Presently she meets the son of a prosperous farmer who lives in the valley below, a fat, freckle-faced lad named Simon, falls in love with him, and imagines she will marry him and lead a normal life.

Then a handsome, powerful preacher comes on the scene

and breaks up her engagement because he believes she is a witch, but of course he falls in love with her. She puts a curse on him and the preacher sickens and nears the point of death. Now she falls in love with him, but the only way she can take the curse off him is to take it upon herself. When she is lying on her deathbed the preacher comes to her well again, and there is a great scene like the one in *Wuthering Heights* where Heathcliff holds Catherine so tightly she is covered with bruises. Charlotte dies and her body is laid out in a house and surrounded by funeral candles. No one will come near because of her powers. "I believed with my soul that this was the work of my life between the ages of fourteen and eighteen," my mother told me. "Later I came to believe that I couldn't do it justice." Slowly she let go of the dream of writing the novel, but did not finally give up on it until she was in university.

She attempted her first short story when she was fifteen, after she'd had her appendix out, but she wasn't able to finish it. Then in grade thirteen she wrote two stories which she did manage to complete. One of these stories used an image that she would pick up on many years later in "Save the Reaper" (*Love*). While she and her mother were driving through the countryside near Wingham they came across a farmhouse whose owner had made mosaics of coloured glass that were set into a wall on his property; odd, dreamlike pictures of human and animal figures, like a Chagall painting. She incorporated the mosaics into her story, the theme of which was art.

Many years later she and Gerry were driving through Bruce County when they accidentally stumbled upon this same farmstead with the mosaic pictures still there in the wall. They stopped to take a look and a strange man who was standing on the property insisted that they come inside, which they agreed to do, against their better judgement. Inside the farmhouse was a scene of the most terrible decrepitude, and a real sense of danger. There were men sitting playing cards in a windowless room and they were terribly drunk. One of them was naked. She and Gerry couldn't wait to get out of there. Later she drew on parts of this experience in "Save the Reaper," when the grandmother finds herself shut in with strangers at a farmhouse, a sinister, almost depraved atmosphere around her.

LITERARY ANCESTORS

Where did my mother's powers come from? Environment certainly played a major role, but so did heredity. Though she did not discover it until she was in midlife, she had Laidlaw ancestors going back as far as the eighteenth century who were renowned for their storytelling abilities and their literary accomplishments. One of these ancestors, Margaret Hogg, had the same extraordinary powers of memory and language that my mother developed. Margaret was the daughter of Will o' Phaup (William Laidlaw), my mother's direct ancestor. He may have been a poor shepherd from the Ettrick Valley in the Scottish Borders, but he was famous, among other things, for being the last man in Scotland to have seen and spoken to the Fairies. She sees him as a "primitive medieval character, like someone from the old sagas: his adventures, his dealings with the supernatural, and his athletic prowess." She loves the accounts that have come down of his sightings of the Fairies, the last one in particular.

"The last time he saw them was very beautiful. He was an old man and he was sitting outside the house and three little boys came along and asked, 'Can you put us up for the night?'

and he said, 'Well, little guys like you, urchins, wouldn't be so hard to find room for,' and then they said, 'Will you give us the key?' and he went in the house looking for the key and then he said to himself, 'What key? I have no key that belongs to them.' Then he turned around, and of course they were gone."

Margaret was famous in the Borders for knowing the Bible by heart and for being a repository for the ballads and stories that had been passed down through the centuries in the oral tradition, many of which she had learned from her father. Such was her reputation that when he was collecting ballads for his *Minstrelsy of the Scottish Border*, Sir Walter Scott came to visit her at her thatched cottage at Ettrick. Despite her misgivings about Scott writing these ballads down – "They were made for singin' and no' for readin'; but ye hae broke the charm noo, an' they'll never be sung mair" – she did recite many of the old ballads to him, some of which are still included in poetry anthologies, and are now part of the Western literary tradition.

Is it too far-fetched to link my mother's near photographic memory to her Laidlaw ancestor? How else can her almost freakish memory, her ability, for instance, to look at her old high-school photos and remember the *colours* of all the dresses the girls are wearing, be explained? And surely her storytelling ability, which so often relates the everyday to the macabre, the nightmare, even the supernatural, the way ballads do, has some affinity with that whole minstrel tradition. The two types of stories came together openly with a Scottish setting in "Hold Me Fast, Don't Let Me Pass" (*Friend of My Youth*), which incorporates a Canadian visitor, Fairies, and the Border landscape.

Margaret Hogg's son was the writer James Hogg, "The Ettrick Shepherd." He was the most famous Scottish poet of his day, next to Burns, and is best remembered for his gothic novel, *Confessions of a Justified Sinner.* Largely forgotten until recent years, it is now considered a masterpiece of its day, and regarded by some critics as superior to anything written by Sir Walter Scott. Despite his background as a poor shepherd with little education (he boasted that he received a total of only three months of schooling), James Hogg made the extraordinary leap from rustic shepherd to celebrated writer, and was fêted in Edinburgh and in London literary circles, where he mixed with the likes of English poets Wordsworth, De Quincey, Southey, and the transplanted Scot, Byron. Besides *Confessions* he published volumes of poetry such as "The Forest Minstrel" and "The Queen's Wake," and a biography of Scott (who was a great friend of his), as well as being a major contributor to *Blackwood's Magazine*, the literary magazine that was shipped out to homesick Britons all over the nineteenth-century Empire. In his last years he was lionized in London, and still publishing books, but when he died in Ettrick in 1835, he was apparently so destitute that he did not even own a pair of shoes. Less than a century separates him from his literary descendant Alice Laidlaw, born in 1931.

CHAPTER 9

Victoria and the Bookstore
1963 –1966

OPENING THE BOOKSTORE

By 1963 my father was taking his dream of opening a book-store seriously, and starting to make plans. Downtown Vancouver wasn't a good location because Duthie's had recently opened, but he didn't want to be in the suburbs, he wanted a central location. It occurred to him that the city of Victoria, on Vancouver Island, was a logical place for a new bookstore. Though still a sleepy town in those days, B.C.'s capital city was starting to open up. A ferry service from the mainland had started in 1960, and a new university, the University of Victoria, had opened its doors in 1962. My father had loved Victoria since his days in the navy: he loved its history, its Victorian architec-ture, its antiquated English charm, and he loved the fact that it received only a third of the rainfall that Vancouver did.

We visited Victoria one weekend in the spring of 1963 to look for a location for the new store, checking in at a motel near the Parliament Buildings, which were lit up at night like a fairy castle. On a previous visit Jenny's comment on the sight had been, "It looks betend." When we arrived it was windy and rainy and I had the impression of a place that was very grey, and very wet. The next day we all trudged around the streets of the downtown as my parents looked for an empty storefront that would be suitable for the new business. We walked and walked until my sister and I grew very tired and my parents had the idea that they would take us to a movie theatre to see a matinee. On Yates Street, we came across an Odeon Theatre, and our parents paid our admission and said they would meet us later. The movie we saw was called *Coffee, Tea or Me?* and it was about stewardesses. I felt very grown up at being able to attend this movie without my parents. While we were watching the flirtatious goings-on of the stewardesses, my parents spotted an empty store right across from the theatre on that covered stretch of Yates Street then known as "the fabulous seven-hundred block." Wedged between Ingledew's Shoes and the Dominion Hotel was 753 Yates Street, the future location of Munro's Book Store.

The store had one of those old-fashioned storefronts, with a recessed entrance flanked by plate-glass display windows. It was long and narrow with a mezzanine above what would be the children's section at the back, and up there my father could have his desk and keep the extra stock. Out the back door there were two mysterious wooden sheds in a tiny yard enclosed by a brick wall, and behind the wall was the Bishop's palace that belonged to St. Andrew's Cathedral around the corner, with its splendid gilded spire. My sister and I didn't know it, but they had already decided to take it.

After our apparently indecisive trip to Victoria I had one more glorious summer in West Vancouver. One more summer of running through the sprinkler, spinning cartwheels on the lawn, building forts in the woods. My parents did not tell us we were moving to Victoria until ten days beforehand. I know this because I remember that after weeping in despair for several minutes upon hearing the announcement I blurted out, "I'll only have ten days to explore the creek." That summer I was exploring farther and farther up the creek, discovering new islands, log-jams, pools where the water ran deep. The move to Victoria took on an apocalyptic significance in my mind. It was the end of the places I loved.

Me, my father, Jenny, and my mother around the time that we moved to Victoria.

Finally my tears tapered off and in the empty calm that followed I came up with the idea of building a mobile of beautiful birds for the new store. That idea sustained me and carried me through to the new life in Victoria, though the reality of the mobile, with its coloured construction-paper birds that would dangle over the children's section in the new store, fell far short of the birds of my imagination. By the time we pulled out of our driveway for the last time I was fatalistic, filled only with vague anticipation as we set the black cat with the kink in its tail free in the woods near the SPCA building, which happened to be closed that day, drove across the Lions Gate Bridge, and said goodbye to West Vancouver forever.

That summer before we moved my father was already in Victoria, preparing the new store for opening: building the fixtures himself, seeing agents, ordering the books, and sleeping on an old mattress in the mezzanine to save money. The figure of two thousand dollars has stuck in my mind as the amount they had saved to put into the business, and I had heard enough to know that their friends back in Vancouver thought they were crazy to take such a risk. The well-known publisher's representative Jim Douglas, who was working for Macmillan at the time, came in and asked him, why Victoria? Concerned, he wanted to know what qualifications my father had to be in the book business, a question that threw him a little. Other people in the business advised him to stock up on books on the Royal Family, gardening, animals, that sort of thing. My father did carry those books, but he was also the first bookseller in Canada to order books from City Lights in San Francisco; so that the beat poetry of Lawrence Ferlinghetti, Allen Ginsberg, and Gregory Corso vied for shelf space with books on growing roses and on Queen Elizabeth. The bookstore described in "The Albanian Virgin" (*Open Secrets*) sounds much like Munro's in the early days.

There was another bookstore, Ford's Books, down Yates Street a couple of blocks, though the main competition came from Eaton's book department. When I won the book prize in grade five for being "the best all-around student," the book I received, *The Marvelous Land of Oz*, came from Ford's and was always tainted because of that. In the nearby Oak Bay neighbourhood (known as being "behind the tweed curtain" because it was so English), Ivy's Bookstore opened a few months after Munro's (Ivy had worked for Duthie's in Vancouver), taking away some of the university crowd my father had hoped to draw on, partly because Ivy let university professors run a line of credit, something my father didn't do, though he did give credit to institutions and to individuals on occasion.

Munro's Book Store opened its doors on September 19, 1963, and on that first day it made over a hundred dollars, an amount that would not be equalled again for a long time afterwards.

Opening day at Munro's, September 1963.

Understandably, business was slow at first (the store made a profit of about two thousand dollars that first year), but my father never had any serious doubts about it succeeding. The books were mostly paperbacks, with fiction titles on one side of the store and non-fiction on the other, with tables displaying hardcovers down the middle and children's books located under the mezzanine at the back. In those days before trade paperbacks, English fiction writers like Evelyn Waugh, Graham Greene, Joyce Cary, and Kingsley Amis were mainly published by Penguin, while popular American books by writers like John Steinbeck, J.D. Salinger, and Kurt Vonnegut, as well as most of the science-fiction and mystery titles, were mass-market publications.

From the beginning, Munro's reflected my father's tastes in all the arts, not just literature, becoming an extension of his personality the way the house in West Vancouver had been. In the window there was a model of a sailing ship he'd had since childhood, and that first Christmas there were panels of the Three Wise Men on a dull-gold background, made by an artist friend in Vancouver, and a tapestry she'd made of a knight on horseback adorned the front of the mezzanine. He played classical records on the record player upstairs, and from the very beginning I always associated the store with Respighi's *Ancient Airs and Dances* and Handel's *Water Music*. Soon he was selling art prints in the store, as well as books; for $3.25 each you could buy reproductions of paintings by the Old Masters: Rembrandt's portraits, Breughel's winter scenes, Picasso's pink and blue harlequins, Degas's dancers.

105 COOK STREET

Our new rented house was a grey stucco bungalow in South Fairfield on the east side of Beacon Hill Park, about a twenty-five-minute walk from downtown. It was then a very ordinary older neighbourhood, now a gentrified preserve where houses have been painted in fashionable shades of grey or green or taupe, with darker trim in hunter green or burgundy or black, where the once plain lawns are now ornamented with trellises and arbours trailing clematis and roses, and where pathways meander among flower beds and ponds. Cook Street ran between South Fairfield and Beacon Hill Park, Victoria's spectacular central park. The boulevard was planted with huge chestnut trees, and we could look out onto the street to a passing parade of old people out walking, tottering on canes. Then, as now, Victoria was a magnet for retired people from all across the country, who were attracted to the mild climate. We used to say Victoria was for "the newly wed and the nearly dead." Across the street were the woods of Beacon Hill Park, and at the end of the street two blocks away was the ocean, where you could look across the Strait of Juan de Fuca to the snowy mountains of the Olympic Peninsula in Washington.

The house had a dining room with French doors, crystal doorknobs, hardwood floors – just the kind of house I would love to live in now. At the time, though, I did not think it compared to the house in West Vancouver, and I was ashamed because we did not have a garage. My father always pulled a U-turn and parked on the street when he came home from the store. I took this as a sign that we were poor.

Upstairs were Jenny's and my bedrooms. The larger one was Jenny's and mine was at the front, a panelled room with sloping walls that looked out on a huge chestnut tree, whose leaves were turning brown around the edges, and the woods of Beacon Hill Park. I loved this room, not least because it had a latch on the door, which meant I could lock Jenny out. I loved being able to run inside, slam the door, and hook the latch just in time when she was chasing me. My mother and I wallpapered Jenny's room one day when she wasn't there. I remember that we got several rolls of French-blue wallpaper for five dollars on sale, and how hard it was to paper all the sloping angles of the ceiling. Jenny tore a strip of the wallpaper off the wall when she got home to show us what she thought of it.

I wasn't always trying to get away from Jenny. At night I used to sneak into her bed and we would take turns scratching each other's backs or tracing someone's face on it with our fingers and making the other guess who it was, or making our hands into shadow puppets on the wall who would peck at each other and get into fights. Sometimes we would prop up our cat Sir Lancelot in the bed and make him gesture with his paws like a puppet king issuing commands. Or else we might take turns being Henry and Martha. Henry would be allotted an inch at the edge of the bed while his loud and obese wife Martha shoved him even further off the bed and berated him if he dared to take an extra inch. Sometimes Henry would trick Martha by sneaking down around Martha's feet and coming up on the other side where there would be all this room. My father used to yell at us to be quiet from the bedroom downstairs, and we would giggle and continue our games in a whisper.

The back garden was hedged by towering holly bushes. It was much smaller than the garden in West Vancouver but not without its own charms: a small rose garden, a pear tree, hyacinths in spring, and orange flowers called calendula every-where in the fall. I pushed Jenny around and around the rows of rose bushes in a wheelbarrow and we tipped our two deck chairs over so they were facing each other, draped a chenille bedspread over them to make a house, and crawled inside to sit on the sweet-smelling grass. The charms of the garden, the park, and the beach were almost enough to compensate for the loss of West Vancouver.

Lately I have begun to have dreams in which I am living in this house again. Sometimes I am living there as a child again, sometimes I am my adult self and I am pleased that my children can have the same life I had. It was a happy time for our family. Perhaps I imagine I can recreate the past and resume my happy life, as you do in dreams. There is always such a buoyant, relieved feeling in the dream, as if everything is right again and I'm back where I belong.

Across from our house on Cook Street, there was the whole of Beacon Hill Park for me and my new friends to explore. Behind the playground across the street were dense thickets of bush crisscrossed by an intricate pattern of paths. Farther still was the fenced enclosure where deer roamed, and peacocks whose cries could be heard at dawn, and the old Clydesdale horse named Queenie. In the park were the tame areas like the ponds where tourists strolled, where we fed the ducks, and the wild areas of slippery, bleached grass and scrubby oak trees behind the old checker house on Beacon Hill with its red and black checker squares painted on the floor. From there you could look across the water to the Olympic Mountains in Washington State and make out the faint outlines of Port Angeles. There was the cricket field, where, if there were a game in progress, we might hear smatterings of applause, and exclamations like "good shot" or "well bowled" from old men with plaid rugs wrapped around their legs even in summer. (My brother-in-law plays cricket on this field today, just as his great-grandfather did after he came out from England in 1860.) There were trees to climb, and woods to explore, though once when we were riding our bikes through the trails by Lovers' Lane, we were stopped by the parks commissioner. "You girls know you shouldn't be in here."

"Why not?" we asked ingenuously.

"You know as well as I do why not."

We did know, vaguely, that there could be perverts lurking in the bushes who might spring out and do something terrible to us.

My mother sometimes took us to the beach at the end of Cook Street, where there was almost always a cool breeze even in summer; I remember the intoxicating fragrance of wild roses, the screen of Garry oaks along the edge of the cliff sculpted to the shape of the wind, the stony beach and the icy water that turned your limbs blue and stung you like needles.

That September Jenny and I started school at Sir James Douglas Elementary. We walked down Faithful Street along an avenue of birch trees that were pure gold and white bark against the deep blue sky of those September days, and zig-zagged our way through the grid of streets of South Fairfield, the boulevards planted with ornamental cherry trees, and the solid two-storey houses closer together and closer to the street than the houses in West Vancouver. I was not happy with my new teacher. She was quite old and she did strange things. Sometimes she was late for school and said she had lost her keys; she fell asleep during film strips; and some days after school she would choose two strong girls, wrap her arms around their shoulders, and be half-escorted, half-dragged to her car. I didn't know it at the time but she was too drunk to walk. A few years later when I was at Central Junior High, I heard that she fell down on the schoolgrounds, was helped up, walked straight into a brick wall, and was taken away for good.

Once we started school and the store opened, our parents' life fell into a new pattern. At first they could not afford to hire anyone to work for them, so my father worked all day and then

again from seven to nine at night to catch the business from
the movie crowd (in a few years the Odeon Theatre across the
street would be attracting big crowds to movies like *Elvira
Madigan*, *A Taste of Honey*, and *Blow-up*). My mother wrote
and did housework in the mornings, and then walked down to
the store to relieve my father for lunch. She worked the afternoon and the Saturday evening shift as well. They came home
at five-thirty to a meal I had prepared, usually pork chops or
sausages or hamburger patties, with mashed potatoes (I was
proud of my mashed potatoes) and boiled peas, beans or corn,
sometimes creamed corn, "mushy gushy" corn, and once in a
while frozen Chinese food heated in the oven. I was an efficient
housekeeper by then, making meals, washing dishes, vacuuming, and sweeping, and my mother was not always happy
about it. Once when she came home from work after I had
cleaned the entire house, inexplicably she burst into tears.

Now that she was working at the store the pressure to write
wasn't so great, and the writing came to her more easily. The
phobias and fears of those last years in West Vancouver had
evaporated along with the gloom of the rainforest. The neighbours were mostly retired people, not at all like "the Monicas"
of the Vancouver suburbs. We'd watch them making their way
along Cook Street with an ancient dignity, dressed in hats and
suits, leaning on canes. They never knocked on our door; they
did not drop by for coffee, or give unsolicited housekeeping
advice, or even ask to borrow a cup of sugar. For that, my
mother was truly grateful. Here, for the first time in her
married life, she was able to sink into the luxury of solitude
and anonymity. The only young person that I knew of was
Ludmilla, a beautiful girl a little older than me, who lived in a

stone house across Faithful Street. She was like a girl in a fairy tale, waving to me from the upstairs casement window as our family walked to the beach at the end of Cook Street. "See, you have friends already," beamed my father. "The beautiful Ludmilla," we called her.

At the store there were a number of "regulars" who came in and talked to my mother. Almost all the regulars were men, and their favourite time to drop by to talk to her was on the Saturday evening shift. They were all characters and she had names for them; one, I remember, was called Marble-Mouth, on account of the incoherence of his speech. They made it hard for her to get any work done, but it was enjoyable for her as well. The store was a place where, for the first time in her

My mother helping customers at the store, around 1965.

life, she could encounter the outside world with confidence, where she could listen to people's stories and then conveniently go home.

Even her shy father in his late thirties had uncovered a dormant sociability that flourished when he began working at the foundry in Wingham, and the camaraderie gave him great satisfaction. It was a huge relief, a liberation, to find oneself socially acceptable after all, after years of seeking to avoid some imagined humiliation. My mother had a similar experience at the store, acquiring a degree of ease and affability she had not possessed before.

Although she wrote only two stories during the Cook Street years, she was happier with her writing than she had been in West Vancouver, especially with the way she could now use personal material from her childhood. She surprised herself by sitting down at her typewriter one day and beginning "Red Dress – 1946" (*Dance*), which she finished in about three weeks. In this story a girl goes to her first high-school dance in the red velvet dress her mother has made for her. She stands alone, undergoing agonizing humiliation as one girl after another is chosen to go out on the dance floor while she is passed by, until the last possible moment, when, just as she is leaving the dance with another girl who also hasn't been asked, salvation appears in the person of classmate Raymond Bolting, blocking her exit, asking her something, asking her to dance.

The other story she wrote while we lived on Cook Street was "Boys and Girls" (*Dance*), with its famous scene of a young farm girl allowing a horse that is to be slaughtered for fox food to escape, opening the farm gate wide instead of closing it when the terrified animal bolts from its would-be executioners.

So many people, especially feminists, wondered about the last line of the story – when the father, referring to her misdeed, pronounces "She's only a girl" – that my mother felt compelled to explain, in a non-fiction article, what she meant. Somehow the position of being a woman, being outside the day-to-day business of making a living, gave a girl, or woman, a perspective that was more authentic, more suited to being a writer. Not a bad thing – at least for someone like her.

"Boys and Girls" was one of her favourite stories, though not her best technically because of a certain disjointed quality she couldn't correct. With this story, going against her usual instinct not to discuss her work, she brought the unpublished manuscript to a creative writing class at UVic at the urging of a friend. One of the group's participants, Lawrence Russell, attacked the story savagely, saying it was something a typical housewife would write. She wasn't able to write anything for about a year after that episode.

AFTER BALLET

I come out of the building into the clear November twilight and walk up Broughton and turn left onto Douglas, Victoria's main street. It is growing dark and the sky is a deep blue and the streetlights with their clusters of glowing globes have come on, but the stores are still open as I walk by them, and the warmth of light inside them is comforting as the mantle of darkness descends over the street. The bright storefronts of the Metropolitan and Woolworth's are cheerful and inviting, the "five and dime" stores where I buy the fine mesh hairnets I need for ballet, and, a few years later, the palest pink lipstick.

Even before I began ballet that September I had heard of Wynne Shaw's reputation. "Some say she carries a stick," is what one of my new friends told me. The first day I attended my new ballet school I was whisked away by Miss Shaw's assistant, her sister, who tied my loose hair in a ponytail before returning me to the class. Soon I learned to do my hair like all the other girls, first making a ponytail on the top of my head, then covering the hair with a hairnet, finally anchoring everything down with lots of bobby pins that scraped your scalp. There was only one mirror in the small room where we all changed into our tights and leotards, and girls would be vying for a position in front of it to do their hair. In the cramped change room there were hooks all around the walls and benches to sit on while you crisscrossed the pink satin ribbon over your ankle, wrapped it around the leg one more time, and tied it behind, tucking in the loose ends. We all wore black leotards and pink tights. Sometimes I would stuff a pair of black tights into my ballet case by mistake and, mortified, I would have to borrow a leotard. In the change room the girls said things like "Really" or "I say" in English accents. They had names like Gillian and Roslyn and they went to private schools.

The studio itself was spacious, with a wall of mirrors across the front, and a barre under a series of arched windows overlooking Victoria's inner harbour. At the barre we practised our pliés and relevés (everything in ballet had French names) while a woman played the piano that was on a raised platform on the other side of the room. In ballet you had to hold your shoulders back, pull up your body, pull in your stomach, and, most important of all, squeeze your bottom under so you would have "turn-out." Turn-out meant having your knees and feet pointing out to the side, preferably at a 180-degree angle. This was necessary so the dancer could move sideways on stage.

No matter how hard I squeezed, my feet would only turn out at a ninety-degree angle and my arches rolled inward. I had to clutch the barre when we lifted one leg to the front, to the side, to the back, higher, higher, higher, until the barre became slippery with sweat under my hand and I could smell the wood. After the barre exercises we formed in rows in the centre of the room and performed arabesques, and pirouettes where you had to twirl around on one foot and twist your head around quickly so you were always looking at the same spot in front of you to keep your balance. At the end of the lesson we executed a formal curtsey to Miss Shaw as if she were the queen.

In the spring we practised for a recital at the Royal Theatre and we had to have a costume, a tutu, made for the occasion. My mother did not sew, she did not even own a sewing machine, so she hired the mother of a friend of mine to do the job. It was to be a red tutu trimmed with gold sequins, and sixteen rows of red net were to be sewn on. When the tutus were finished we had to model them for Miss Shaw. My costume was singled out, there was something wrong with the way the layers of net had been sewn on; they had to be taken off and sewn on again. Somehow I had known this would happen.

In my second year my ballet humiliations became more severe. We all got toe shoes and had to darn the blocky ends of the shoes with pink thread and stuff the ends with cotton wool. While all the other dancers made mincing little steps across the studio on their toe shoes, I remained at the barre, clinging to it like a life raft as I stiffened my body and leapt onto the ends of my toes in an effort to be weightless. Sometimes when I took off my slippers afterwards, my toes would be bleeding. In the months before the ballet examinations, Miss Shaw made me take an extra class every week so that I would not disgrace her by failing. I didn't fail, but I wasn't highly recommended or even recommended at all; I merely passed, but even so I was tremendously relieved.

Now I see myself turning down Yates Street under the covered sidewalk, past Sweet Sixteen, Standard Furniture, Ingledew's Shoes, until I arrive under the sign that says Munro's Book Store. Beneath the mezzanine is the children's section, books of fairy tales, *The Sleeping Beauty*, *Cinderella*, a rack of *How and Why* books, *Orlando the Marmalade Cat*, *Pookie*, the bunny with fairy wings, and idiotic little Noddy wearing his pointed cap. Above the children's section hangs the bird mobile I made, coloured construction-paper cut-outs dangling from pieces of black thread. At the very back is a little space with a bathroom on one side and a coat closet on the other, a table for unpacking the books that come in, for checking them against the invoices and pricing them before putting them on the shelves, and for wrapping up the books that are to be returned to the publishers.

Upstairs in the mezzanine is my father's desk. There's an old mattress on the floor and in one corner a record player and piles of my father's records. Periodically he stacks three or four records above the turntable and turns the switch to automatic. The first record drops to the turntable, and the arm with the needle lifts up, moves over and drops down to the edge of the record. After the first record is over, the process repeats itself until all the records have played. Then he turns the stack over and plays the other sides. I stretch out on the mattress and read a book, trying to ignore the knot of tears in the back of my throat until my father closes the store and we go home for dinner.

JOANN

In grade six I became best friends with JoAnn, a girl from my class who lived at the end of Faithful Street. We met through a mutual friend, Susan, a large, meek-looking girl, and the three of us took to playing dress-up in her basement, or staging battles with her brother Glen, who pelted us with rocks from behind his barricades in their backyard. Jo became my counterpoint to the world of ballet and drama classes and being taken to the symphony by my father on Sunday afternoons. We preferred to play badminton, or double-ride our bikes, or listen to the Beatles' *Rubber Soul* in JoAnn's bedroom after school. My father did not approve of my new friendship in the way that he had approved of Anne back in West Vancouver. He knew she was taking me away from him. JoAnn was not pretty and refined like Anne; she was short, stocky, pug-nosed, and outrageous. She made up names for everyone; various classmates of ours were "queeros" and "weirdos," her silent father was "monosyllabic," Donna Porteous became "Donna Pottomous," Joanne Koblinsky was "J.K." We would knock on the door of our house pretending we were beggars, and my mother would open the door. "Help the hungry Hoopers" we'd cry, rattling empty tin cans. "Save the mental Munros." My mother would throw her head back and laugh, the only adult to be delighted with our antics.

There is a beach JoAnn and I go to, a crescent of sand bounded by outcroppings of rock at either end. We are unable to swim in the freezing water but we scour the beach for suitable logs or planks and float around on them, using broad sticks for paddles, exploring the sandy coves, skirting rocks scored and gouged by glaciers.

One day I am at this beach, not with JoAnn but with my father, who is never happier than when at the beach lying face down with a book propped up in front of him, sitting up periodically to baste himself with baby oil. My mother never enjoyed lying in the sun. Sometimes my father made her lie under our sunlamp under the mistaken impression that it would be good for her varicose veins. This afternoon I am paddling around on a log with a boy of about my own age who has suddenly befriended me. It is partly a childhood friendship, partly a flirtation. The boy invites me to come and meet a friend of his on the beach. His friend is an older man sitting crosslegged on a patch of sand surrounded by logs. He is completely bald and his tanned scalp shines in the sun. There is something wrong about the way this man is talking to me. Before I leave the beach to go home, the boy gets my phone number.

That evening the phone rings and I pick it up. It is the man from the beach and he wants me to go and meet him in Lovers' Lane in the park. I say I can't, my mother wouldn't allow me to go. He says my mother doesn't have to know. I tell him no, very politely, and hang up the phone. My mother has been listening from the kitchen, and when I tell her what the man said she calls the police and an officer comes to the house. The officer takes down a description of the man, but says there's really nothing he can do.

At about this time, I am walking along Cook Street in my new orange lace-up bell-bottoms, when a car coming up behind me slows down. I think the man in the car wants to ask for directions, but he doesn't stop. I realize with a tiny shock inside that he has slowed down to look at me, the same way that my father slows down when he is driving past a girl walking on the sidewalk, and cranes his neck around to see if her face is pretty.

CHAPTER 10

Rockland

1966 –1973

MOVING TO ROCKLAND

One day we came home from school for lunch and were eating the pan-fried potatoes my mother made for us every day, and she said she had something to tell us. Could we guess what it was? "Mrs. Ross is having another baby," I said. The Rosses were friends of ours who at that time had six children. "No. I am. I'm the one who is going to have another baby." The year was 1966 and I was twelve and my sister Jenny eight, and our mother was thirty-five. She looked pleased, even though she did confide to us some years later, *sotto voce*, "Not enough jelly on the diaphragm."

That summer we had to leave our rented house; I believe the owners wanted to move back in. I was lying on the living-room floor looking through the "Houses for Sale" section in the Want Ads when I spotted an advertisement for a house on Rockland Avenue. The Rockland neighbourhood was up the hill from South Fairfield, where there were turn-of-the-century mansions in Tudor, or Georgian, or Victorian design, surrounded by sweeping lawns and flower beds, enclosed by stone walls. My father and I drove up Rockland Avenue to take a look at this house, discovering that it was far grander than anything I had known before. The house was built in the exposed-beam mock-Tudor style with a bay window, a verandah, and French doors opening onto a balcony upstairs. There was a stone wall dividing the half-acre property from the street and two stone turrets on either side of a long, narrow driveway. On the grounds were Garry oaks, and other trees I could not name, and at the end of a little path were two empty ponds and an ivy-covered gazebo. At this time the house was being used as a duplex and it needed work. The front porch was falling down and the whole house required a top-to-bottom paint job. The owners were in some kind of financial trouble, which must have been why they accepted my father's low offer.

That summer my mother was fairly incapacitated by the advanced state of her pregnancy, and so was more acquiescent than usual. I knew she did not want to live in such a house, but my father and I were so keen on having it that she did not protest very much. As a token of resistance, she said she would move to the house on one condition: I would have to do all the vacuuming. (I was twelve, but I kept my end of the bargain, spending three hours every Saturday morning at the task while she was working at the store.)

Once again my father and I were brought together by our common desire to live in a house like this, as we had been brought together in loving the house in West Vancouver. "It has five fireplaces," we told people. "It has twelve-foot ceilings; there are two staircases and a maids' quarters." Upstairs there were five bedrooms: a master bedroom with a fireplace, Jenny's room, the two bedrooms that made up the maids' quarters, and the "workroom," the old upstairs kitchen from when the house had been a duplex. In the workroom there was a washing machine, a dryer and an ironing board, and soon there was my mother's typewriter, on the old dining-room table from West Vancouver. This room was where she did all her writing; it was where she wrote *Lives of Girls and Women*. After we moved in, my father gave all our visitors "the grand tour," whether they asked for it or not. Of course we did not give much thought to the upkeep that such a house would require. We did not concern ourselves with mundane matters like housework.

At the end of August we moved into the new house and a few days later, on September 8, 1966, the same day that I started high school, my sister Andrea Sarah was born. Andrea was to

My mother holding Andrea, beside my grandfather Laidlaw at the house on Rockland Avenue, Victoria, in 1966.

have been an Andrew but my mother knew all along that she would have another girl. She wanted an old-fashioned name like Charlotte or Sarah, but I was the one who chose Andrea. (My mother had wanted to give me an exotic name like Deirdre or Maeve, but my father would not hear of it.) We did not go up to her room at the Royal Jubilee Hospital. My father parked on the street and we waved to her as she held the baby up to the window. I had prepared for the baby's arrival by making a basket for her to sleep in, a wicker basket with blue and pink satin ribbons woven through it.

To furnish the new house, my father had the massive dining-room suite that had belonged to his grandparents sent out from Ontario, re-covering the chairs in green leather. Above the table he installed a brass chandelier like the ones in Vermeer paintings, and hung framed prints of El Greco's *View of Toledo*, and the dreamlike Chagall painting my mother loved, *I and the Village*. The hallway to the side entrance was converted into "the chapel," to house the new church organ my father played on Sundays, and the windows around the door were painted with medieval motifs in jewel colours to look like stained glass. In time the garden was adorned with statuary, an angel rising from the rock garden where the poppies grew, and a little statue of Pan crouching on top of a bird bath, which was stolen one night. I planted tulips in the fall and rows of marigolds and geraniums in spring, but the flowers languished in the dusty soil of rain-free Victoria, and ours was the only lawn on the street allowed to go brown in summer. We used to joke that the guides on the double-decker buses going by would quickly point out some scenic landmark on the other side of the street so the tourists' gaze would be averted from the sight of our yard.

It was never really a comfortable house. In the winter it was never adequately heated, since the heat was always off at night and the radiators wouldn't even get warm until late afternoon, when our cat would regularly drape herself over one of them for her nap. My father worried so much about the heating bills that if my mother had the heat turned up high during the day, she would open all the doors before he got home so he wouldn't know. We took a lot of hot baths in the claw-footed tub upstairs just to get warm.

After Andrea was born, my mother was very tired, more tired than she had been with Jenny and me, when she was in her twenties. Later she spoke of coming home from work and being so busy that she would be in the house for half an hour before having a chance to take her coat off. I remember her nursing Andrea in the bedroom; I came in and heard the feeding noises and told her it was disgusting. She gave up on nursing soon after that.

Later that fall my mother went back to working at the store on Saturdays, and my job, besides doing all the vacuuming on Saturday mornings, was to look after Andrea. I changed her on a towel on my parents' bed (it never occurred to anyone to have a change table), trying not to stab her with the big safety pins; bounced her in the Jolly Jumper; put her down in her crib for her nap. I never told anyone this, but once I neglected to secure the gate at the top of the back stairs (the maid's stairs that went down to the kitchen), and when I was cleaning the kitchen I heard the ka-thunk, ka-thunk, ka-thunk as she rolled sideways all the way down those steep, wooden stairs. I held my breath but then she started crying and I knew she was all right, and not seriously injured.

Andrea and Jenny in front of the Rockland Avenue house.

DANCE OF THE HAPPY SHADES

In 1968 my mother published her first collection of short stories, *Dance of the Happy Shades*. The idea for the collection came from Earle Toppings, who was the editor of Ryerson Publishers at the time. He wrote to her suggesting that if she could write three more stories, she would have enough material for a book. Of course, publishing a collection of short stories was something she had been trying to do since 1961, when she had written to Jack McClelland. Now in her mid-thirties, she had been writing the stories that were collected in *Dance* for close to fifteen years. The stories included from the North Vancouver years were "The Shining Houses" (*Anthology*), and two from *Chatelaine*, "The Time of Death" and "Day of the Butterfly" (originally published as "Good-by Myra"). The five stories she wrote during her seven years in West Vancouver were all collected. They were "The Peace of Utrecht" (*The Tamarack Review*), four stories from *The Montrealer*: "Dance of the Happy Shades," "An Ounce of Cure," "The Office," and "A Trip to the Coast," along with the two stories she wrote when we lived on Cook Street, "Red Dress – 1946" and "Boys and Girls" (both from *The Montrealer*). The three stories she completed to round off the collection, "Postcard" (*The Tamarack Review*), "Images," and "Walker Brothers Cowboy," were all composed in the workroom in the house on Rockland Avenue, where for the first time she had a room of her own.

"It was a great thing when I got the room upstairs at Rockland. I didn't have to tidy up – there was all my stuff in front of me.

Front cover of
Dance of the Happy Shades
(Ryerson Press, 1968).

I had a nice view. It was a good room to write in." She kept her manuscripts in a round black tin she kept in a cupboard drawer.

When I think of the story "Images," I see the man coming through the woods swinging a hatchet, and I remember the girl's reaction when she sees him, how what hits her "did not feel like fear so much as recognition." "Images" is one of my mother's favourite stories, and is fairly autobiographical. At first she wrote it as a poem in one of those spiral-bound scribblers she kept. In her round loopy handwriting, she envisioned "A man bare-headed like a speckled egg/Carrying a little axe/A hatchet, which he swung like a toy/And he came on, gleeful, silent."

She has also written an essay about the story that for me comes closer than anything else of hers I've read to describing the process of creating fiction, or at least closer to how she created fiction. It did begin with the image of the man with the hatchet coming down the riverbank, with her father unaware because he is bending over his muskrat traps. "From this picture the story moved outward, in a dim, uncertain way. When this happened I was not so much making it as remembering it. I remembered the nurse-cousin, although there was nobody to remember, no original for her. I remembered the trip along the river, to look at traps with my father, although I never went. I remembered my mother's bed in the dining-room, although it was never set up there."

I can understand the process this way, as if you are remembering things that did not actually happen, in the way that you remember dreams perhaps. You may be standing at the kitchen sink and a whole scene from last night's dream, with its moods, and complications, and characters, will suddenly flash before you and fill you with its own particular truth, and you can't believe you could have forgotten it.

MOTHER AND FRIEND

Q: Do your daughters accept you as an individual apart from their mother? Does it embarrass them to think of you, in your books as a sexually active woman who falls in and out of love, who reveals her weaknesses? Do they resent not getting a "normal" mother?

A: I've found when they become teenagers, there's been total acceptance of me, and it's just a marvelous thing – the friendship I have with the two girls and I hope I'll have with the younger one. If they still have any embarrassment, they gallantly keep it from me.

– from an interview with Kem Murch,
Chatelaine magazine, August 1975

My mother in 1968.

A bout the time when we moved into the new house when I was thirteen, my mother and I began to be more like girl-friends than like mother and daughter. It was 1966, and we both favoured the lacy stockings and shorter skirts that came into fashion that year. She advised me to dye my hair blonde, which I did, and I cut her hair in layers. We shared clothes, or at least I felt free to borrow her clothes, and we both shopped at Sweet Sixteen. One Christmas I made matching dresses for us, trimmed with gold sequins, mine made of beige wool, hers, more successfully, of green velvet. She listened to my Beatles records and we discussed whether Nowhere Man was God. My father preferred the irony of songs like "She's Leaving Home" on *Sergeant Pepper's Lonely Hearts Club Band*, the album I played incessantly all through the summer of 1967. Not usually as sympathetic to the music I played as my mother was, he had only been won over to the Beatles by the trumpet solo at the end of "Penny Lane." If I was playing one of my non-Beatles records, maybe Crosby, Stills and Nash, or James Taylor, or The Byrds, and I didn't see his car in time, he would take off the record and stomp through the music room, glaring at me and my friends as if we had committed some capital offence.

My mother fed books to me the way other mothers fed food, as essential nourishment. I was proud that she recommended *Lolita* to me at the age that Lolita is in the novel, thirteen. I remember sitting on the front steps with my mother and her friend Sally, and how Sally said she didn't like Nabokov's writing, she thought it was pretentious. I found it interesting, amazing even, to discover that people could dare to have these opinions about literature. In those years I devoured the novels my mother passed along to me, among them *A Tree Grows in Brooklyn*, *Doctor Zhivago*, and *War and Peace*, and non-fiction titles like *The Feminine Mystique* and *The Second Sex*.

I remember our conversation at The Old House Restaurant again, when we were talking about how she saw herself as a mother at that time, how determined she was to be as different from her own mother as possible. That was when she summarized her approach with the words "Let's say I was thinking of the kind of mother I would be, not what it would do to you."

In her view it wasn't so much when we were young children growing up in West Vancouver, or even in those first years in Victoria, that this hands-off approach to motherhood became a problem. It was only in the late sixties, she believes, when my emergence into adolescence coincided with the explosion of the counterculture, that she felt it wasn't good for us, that she had failed us in some way.

Me, my father, and my mother in 1968. (photo by Irve Kuusk)

"In retrospect I think I probably didn't establish nearly enough distance, didn't establish enough of a mother's authority, so that it left you dangling without this natural reference point. And then especially as you grew up into adolescence

I hated the image of the mother who disapproved of every-thing, who had a different set of values, the mother who was at the ironing board. It was the refusal to sink into this role which made me self-centred instead of thinking about what you could have used. I should have been telling you, I should have been teaching you.

"I was into my own role but this had to be seen through the tremendous change of values that came in the late sixties and that split women of my age. Some women decided to go against it, some women decided to be like their mothers. I wanted to be as if I were ten years younger. With the women of thirty-five, women born in the early nineteen-thirties, there was a big problem about how to be an adult in this period, not only because the prejudice against adults was so firm (Abbie Hoffman saying anyone over thirty couldn't be trusted) but also so justified in my eyes. The times had a lot to do with the kind of mother I was to you and Jenny [then], but not earlier. There it was more to let you be yourselves but it was also to let me be myself so I wasn't engaged with the terribly serious busi-ness of making you into the kind of people I thought you should be. I didn't have any notions about that. We were all in this adventure."

As a mother of two boys, in many ways I am like her, leaning towards freedom and self-expression, and encouraging a scep-tical attitude towards the status quo without a lot of emphasis on rules, limits, moral guidance. At times I feel perilously close to abdicating my role as a parent. My own distrust of authority and institutions and most of the popular culture is being passed on to them. Encouraging individual freedom of thought and expression in them is more important to me than ensuring that they fit into conventional society. I do not want them to conform, but as a parent I wonder whether conforming, believing in the structures they are given, will make them into happier, more well-adjusted adults.

THE COUNTERCULTURE

M unro's in the late sixties became something of a mecca for Victoria's counterculture. It was the first establishment in Victoria to sell personality posters, black-and-white blow-ups of twentieth-century icons: W.C. Fields, Charlie Chaplin, Marilyn Monroe, Pierre Elliott Trudeau with a rose in his teeth, soon followed by psychedelic posters with their fluorescent colours and swirling patterns. Munro's had art nouveau bookmarks, including one designed by my mother and one of the staff members with a drawing of a girl looking sadly into a mirror and the caption, "Seduced and Abandoned? Relax with a book from Munro's." There were all kinds of books on Eastern philosophy and religion, astrology, palmistry, handwriting analysis, even *Psychic Discoveries Behind the Iron Curtain*. There were books on macrobiotic cooking and hand-made houses, yoga, and meditation, and Kahlil Gibran's *The Prophet*, often quoted reverentially at weddings. The novels of Hermann Hesse, Kurt Vonnegut, Ken Kesey, and Tolkien sold by the hundreds. When I was working at the store I remember one discussion about whether we should have to pay customs duty on a marijuana-growing handbook, because it was a how-to book, and how-to books were supposedly exempt. The one counterculture title my father refused to carry, for obvious reasons, was *Steal This Book* by Abbie Hoffman.

In 1967 I went to Centennial Square in downtown Victoria

Munro's staff party at the house on
Rockland, late 1960s. I am on the far right,
Andrea and Jenny in the front.

by City Hall. It was famous for being the place where the
hippies hung out, to the consternation of the municipal officials;
one alderman went as far as to suggest that the hippies should
be driven out of the square with whips. Costumed in my new
dress-up clothes, a pair of tight paisley bell-bottoms I had
sewn, sandals, beads made out of rolled-up strips of magazines,
dyed blonde hair swinging below my shoulders, I went down
there, hoping to meet hippies. I was sitting on the edge of the
fountain when a young man with long hair (a notable drug
dealer in Victoria, I later found out) came up to me, bent over,
and kissed me on the lips. It was an ecstatic moment, like the
moment in *Lives of Girls and Women* when Garnet French
touches Del's hand in the Baptist church. It was an affirmation
of the power I had.

I sought out that kind of moment but I was never really part
of the hippie crowd at all. I was very timid about taking drugs,
and I didn't know how to join in with the hippies who hung

out in Centennial Square or at the cafeteria in the basement of the Hudson's Bay Company, or at The Nine in the Fifth Place (the club named after the hexagrams in the *I Ching*). I was flirting around the edges of things but I never took the kinds of risks or flouted authority the way they did.

A year or so later my friend Audrey (JoAnn was now a boarder at a private school, and we no longer saw each other) and I rolled a joint in my bedroom and smoked it right then and there. We had my mother's permission. As we sailed out the door on our way to the youth centre downtown, she called out to us, "Save a joint for me." She was not like other mothers and I was proud of her for that, not to mention a little jealous of the way she charmed all my friends.

A few months later, she changed her mind. The child of friends of theirs from the Unitarian church had died of an overdose; around the same time someone at my high school died after sniffing glue. A chill descended over the whole idea of my experimenting with drugs. After that I hid the signs of being stoned as best I could. When I came home after smoking a joint, I would go directly upstairs to my bedroom and wave my hair over a stick of incense to try to mask the smell. Unlike other parents, mine knew what marijuana smelled like. They had friends who smoked it all the time and they went to parties where a joint might be passed around, where they might discuss Timothy Leary's theories about the virtues of LSD.

"A WOMEN'S LIB TYPE"

I sensed that sexual experimentation was not something my mother disapproved of, and I knew this was true once *Lives of*

Girls and Women came out. How could a mother who wrote of the sexual encounters between Del and Garnet French, and of Del's rebellion against her mother's anti-sex stance, not want her own daughter to be free? She did want me to be free, but at the same time she was worried, and so she sent me mixed messages. She didn't tell me not to have sex, but she warned me about the possibility of having a back-street abortion in Seattle. This was in 1970, when I was sixteen, and it was still illegal to have an abortion in Canada. It was the year before I went on the Pill.

My father was the one who really worried about me. He'd see me traipsing off to school in one of my miniskirts and he'd yell after me, "You're not going to school dressed like that, are you?" Of course he could not stop me. Once he spotted me walking home from school arm-in-arm with a boyfriend of mine, and he reported to my mother, "They were hugging on the street." It seemed that he was always trying to shame me. He was the one who would veto my requests to go out to clubs or sleep over at my girlfriend Robyn's house. While her parents were working as Baha'i missionaries in Samoa, Robyn shared an apartment with an older brother whose phrase of choice was "Far fuckin' out," and who believed that people who owned homes were "capitalist pigs." It was not quite true, as my father suspected, that there were "wild sex orgies" going on, but there were drugs. I remember one particularly unpleasant episode when I found myself looking down a toilet bowl after smoking a joint and drinking from a bottle of Grand Marnier that was passed around as a chaser.

My boyfriends admired my mother and confided in her. I remember one of them, who appealed to me partly because he had spent time in Haney Correctional Institution for the possession of heroin, and sent me letters from jail saying "i luv u," sitting with me and my mother at our kitchen table telling her about his designs on me. "Yes, I'm after her body," he told her, "but I'm after her mind too," as I sat there, the mute object of desire, silenced by pride and shame. She nodded with under-standing, as if this were just another story a friend was telling her.

At the grand house on Rockland Avenue my parents gave parties. My father was now serving Black Russians, a potent mix of Tia Maria and vodka. There were staff parties, Victoria Day parties where everyone had to dress up in Victorian cos-tumes, and parties after the gruelling process of stock-taking at the store was over. The friends they entertained were Unitarians,

Victoria Day party at Rockland Avenue, 1971.
Back row: Elizabeth Pinn, Mary Duthwaite, me.
Front row: Jerri Jelinek, my father, Jenny.

teachers, customers, and occasionally writers. Margaret Atwood came to the house once with her husband and charted my horoscope. Apparently my childhood was going to have a huge impact on my life. Audrey Thomas stayed with us, and she and my mother have remained close friends ever since. At one of the parties they gave I was dancing, in a peasant dress with a tight bodice and black lace-up boots, when I caught the attention of the son of friends of my parents, who was a few years older than I, in his early twenties. Later he invited me to spend a weekend with him at a place in the country where some friends of his lived. I remember my mother was standing at the bottom of the stairs, waffling about letting me go, but he talked her into it in the most charming way. When we arrived at the friends' home we walked around a lake together and I found myself completely paralysed, unable to utter a single word. The next morning before he awakened I escaped from the house and made it to the highway, where I hitched a ride home.

As a teenage girl I was not prepared for this intoxicating freedom, this lack of limits (the opposite of the "love of limits" of the fifties). I wanted to be like Del but I did not have the saving grace of being a writer. As my mother's daughter, coming of age at the end of the sixties, bolstered by the women's movement and the availability of the Pill, and seduced by the whole mystique of the counterculture, how could I have been otherwise?

I'm looking at a photo of my mother taken in 1972 or 1973. She is standing in the living room of the house on Rockland Avenue with the tall panels of the bay window behind her. The photo is part of the article "Great Dames," by Barbara Frum. It profiles other notable Canadian women besides my mother: a painter, a photographer, a student. These are women, says Frum, "who won't fit their lives into the chinks and spaces left around by the demands of their children and their men." She tells us confidently, "every nation in the West is now allowing women to own up to ambition and a craving for recognition and achievement."

Ah, the rhetoric of the women's liberation movement. It all comes back to me, the way that women, at least liberated women, felt this buoyant optimism about how they could transform their lives if only they could shuck the chains of oppressive institutions that bound them. The women in the article talked about how they weren't playing games any more, how they weren't trying to please, they were refusing to be "nice." My mother said that she was changing; where she used to act charming when she disagreed with a man, now she would argue. For women who were older it was better to look a little weird, she thought, to have hair with a few streaks of grey in it, than it was to be "embalmed." The idea was to strip away things, make-up, material possessions, masks, games, and get to the true self that would reveal itself. This was the hope, the belief, the religion. I had forgotten how radical it was, how idealistic the women's liberation movement was before the whole question of feminism was divested of its vision, and stripped down to a matter of economics and "having choices," and personal freedom came to mean having the mortgage paid off and being able to take early retirement. Then, the emphasis was on how women could reinvent themselves, create something new, not just have an equal share of the pie that men have.

My grade twelve history teacher made the radical move of having us move all of our desks so that we faced each other in a semi-circle. As a technique he would throw out provocative questions to get discussions going, a gambit that rarely succeeded with our class, usually having the opposite effect of keeping us as silent as the grave. On one occasion he went around the room pointing to each girl in succession, "Are you a woman's lib type?" he asked, and on to the next, "Are you a woman's lib type?" and each girl looked down and shook her head in meek submission, until he got to me. "Yes," I replied, throwing down the gauntlet, and my girlfriend Linda, sitting next to me, my only ally, said "Yes" also. After class he remonstrated with us, "But don't you want to be put on a pedestal? Isn't that what women want?" "No, I do not," was all I could manage; my heart was pounding so hard I was shaking. How could I make him understand that his condescension was just the problem? That being on the pedestal meant we had no real power? That was in 1971, when the women's movement was really gearing up. At home I began referring to my father as the MCP, short for Male Chauvinist Pig.

That was the year I read Germaine Greer's *The Female Eunuch.* I can still see the striking jacket image – the metal cast of a woman's torso with handles on either side – on its shelf near the back of the store. I was working at Munro's on Saturdays by then, and I remember, during tea breaks at the back of the store, we would talk about the merits of keeping our own names when we got married, about having our own money, about equal pay for equal work. To entertain each other we read out passages from retrograde books like *Fascinating Womanhood* and *The Total Woman* at the cash desk between customers, about how the feminine woman should greet her husband at the door wrapped in Saran Wrap, that kind of thing. There weren't any men on staff in those early years. At the store my father didn't miss the opportunity to surround himself with lovely, intelligent, young women, several of whom became close personal friends of both my parents. Far from being jealous, my mother enjoyed their wit and liveliness and irreverence as much as he did. My father did put a premium on looks, though. He was never one to love you for your self alone, and not your yellow hair. In a book he kept for jotting down notes about potential employees he had interviewed, I saw comments like "Good-looking!" in the margins. There were two Elaines working at the store; one he called "the fair Elaine," while the other was just Elaine, who was quite attractive, too. I wondered how she felt about that.

LIVES OF GIRLS AND WOMEN

After the success of *Dance of the Happy Shades*, for which she received the Governor General's Award in 1968 (an extraordinary year, when other winners included Mordecai Richler, Leonard Cohen, and Marie-Claire Blais), my mother had a very hard time getting started again. She didn't write anything at all for about a year and a half.

Then, quite suddenly, at the end of 1969, she began work on a novel, "a conventional coming-of-age novel." She began it one Sunday after my father told her to go down to the bookstore and lock herself in so she could write. He said he would make dinner and look after my sisters and me. Alone in the empty store, at first she felt oppressed by all the books surrounding her, all those great works of literature reproaching her, but then she did begin to write. It was the beginning of the Princess Ida chapter, the one about Del's mother going on the road selling encyclopedias and Del reeling off the names of all the presidents of the United States to prospective buyers, which would become part of *Lives of Girls and Women*. Her first sentence was, "My mother sold encyclopedias." (Is it significant that once again she begins with the mother and daughter theme, the mother who is trying hard to be enterprising and the daughter who is embarrassed by her, and recalcitrant?)

After that Sunday in the bookstore my mother began to write every day. (Since that time she has been able to write most of the time, for several hours each day, without periods of writer's block, and without abandoning stories and novels as she had done in her earlier years.) She was happy all that winter. On her way to pick up three-year-old Andrea from the play school called "Auntie Mary's," she would walk by a certain house that had its Christmas lights up until some time in February, and she would think, "The lights are still up and I've written so much, not much time has passed and I've done all this writing."

In March she was sitting politely in the middle of a luncheon for another writer when it suddenly struck her that this piece of writing she was doing was "a disaster." She realized that by following a strictly chronological progression she would never get it to work, that she had no "authority" over the material. What she had to do was to reorganize everything so it was clustered around themes. There would be a section on death, another on religion, one on the mother, one on sexual excitement (the operettas performed at school) and "the heavy sexual thing" that was "Baptizing." Of course this is largely why the novel has the feel of a collection of interrelated stories; themes are dealt with one at a time rather than being interwoven throughout. She described to me how she needed a "separate tension" in each section, how there had to be "some kind of build and a summing up" in each.

After she worked on the manuscript all through the winter and spring of 1970, my mother, my father, and I (I was sixteen) went to Ireland for three weeks that summer. Jenny, who at thirteen was too embarrassed by her parents to want to go anywhere with them, chose to stay at Rockland under the care of

Irve from the bookstore, whom she considered "cool," while Andrea stayed at a playschool. My get-up for Ireland was a tartan miniskirt (even though my mother warned me that miniskirts wouldn't be allowed in Ireland) and a stretchy lace top. Miniskirts were allowed, and so was drinking for minors. I drank Guinness with my parents in pubs across the land, from Limerick, to Cork, to Dublin, and back across the country to Galway and Sligo, and there was never any problem. We ventured over to the Aran Islands one blustery wet day and had to have Irish whisky in the hold of the ship to revive us on our way back. In the Yeats country around Sligo, we visited the tower where Yeats lived, signed on for a tour of Lisadell House, where beautiful Maud Gonne had lived, conducted by her decrepit Anglo-Irish descendants (my mother noted the bits of food that had dribbled onto our guide's shirt), and even rowed to the Lake Isle of Innisfree. We saw the church at Cashel where the Catholics seeking sanctuary had been burned inside and felt the "bad vibes" of the place, and stopped at the monastic beehive dwellings at Glendalough dating back to the sixth century. More than the history of the place, I remember my mother saying that you come to a place like this and all you might be thinking is, "I really need to go to the bathroom."

Once, somewhere in the middle of the country, a place where there were swans on a river, when I had to come back to my parents' room because I had forgotten the key to my room, I caught my mother weeping, obviously in the middle of a fight with my father. She was angry at me for finding her like that, and pretended nothing was wrong.

When my mother got back from Ireland she couldn't find her manuscript. For a few terrible minutes, as she was ransacking the house, she thought the cleaning lady must have thrown it out.

Then she remembered where she had carefully hidden it. (My mother has been known to throw her royalty cheques away, and I have seen her rummaging through the garbage in desperation on at least one occasion.) Working steadily over the fall, she was able to complete the manuscript and rewrite it once before Christmas 1971. (In these days before computers, changing something neatly could mean retyping the entire manuscript, so in order to avoid the problem she performed some "amazing acrobatics." If she put in a new line she would find a line she could delete on that same page. That way she wouldn't have to retype the entire manuscript. I don't think it would have occurred to her to insert extra pages and number them 1A, 2A and so on.)

I have an outline that she made for the novel, written in red and blue pencil crayons, which must have been drawn up that winter. In her broad loopy script she has made a list:

Plan-Novel

1. Intro-Encyc
2. Mr. C & F.D. Sx
3. Mother
4. Operetta & Rel
5. Operetta Perf & Rel (Easter)
6. Spring-Boat – Mr. C.
7. Boat-Mr. C. Letters Car
8. 24th May-book Letter
9. SxE.
10. Mr. C gone F.D. conf (LGW)
11. Movingback-Uncle Benny-book
12. Visit

13. Suicide
14. Funeral
15. Fin.

The section that gave her the most difficulty, the one she worked on "about six times as hard as the rest of the novel," was the book's epilogue, "The Photographer." At first she didn't believe she could bring herself to do it – to end with Del growing up to be the writer looking back and trying to make sense of her experience – thinking it would be "boring and clichéd." Then, once she started working on it, she found she couldn't leave it out. She was writing and rewriting it over several months, even sending off another "final" last page after the manuscript had been mailed to the publishers.

The novel was finished in June of 1971, at the time I graduated from high school, about the same age Del was when she failed to win the scholarship to university; it was published by McGraw-Hill Ryerson in the fall of that year. (Originally my mother had wanted to call the novel *Real Life*, but decided not to after coming across a recent American novel with that title.) The release of *Lives* brought her immediate recognition and critical acclaim. Critics (male critics) praised it, but were quick to point out that it wasn't a masterpiece, its achievement was "small but fine," it may not challenge us but it "satisfies our expectations." I sense there was an understanding that there was another kind of fiction, the fiction of big ideas, of moral struggle, a panoramic picture of society, that was regarded as being on a higher plane; the realistic novel was a lesser achievement. No matter how beautifully rendered, the "ordinary" world she brought into being was somehow of a lower order. And though they didn't say it, the term "woman's writer" came to mind.

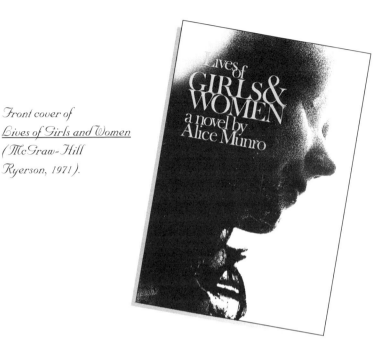

Front cover of
Lives of Girls and Women
(McGraw-Hill
Ryerson, 1971).

She sent a copy of the new book to her father, and in a letter dated Sunday, November 21, 1971, he gave her his assessment:

> *You will wonder of course if I "like" it. I don't think it's a case of liking it but more of accepting it as a fact of life. This is a powerful book and very strong medicine indeed. I sometimes wished that you had not been quite so explicit in the matter of sex but then you have set out to write of a young girl's growing-up, her reaction to life and to that very important part of life, sex. . . . I suppose your book could be considered another weapon in the freeing of women from the cant and hypocrisy of the double standard. It is fortunate to be coming out when women's Lib is to the fore.*

LIVES OF GIRLS AND WOMEN – THE EPILOGUE

In the Epilogue, the final chapter in *Lives of Girls and Women*, Del begins writing a Gothic novel after high school, the kind of novel whose heroine has "bittersweet flesh, the color of almonds." She uses a real family in Jubilee, the Sheriff family, as a starting point, but transforms the material to the point where the original Sheriff family becomes virtually unrecognizable. Then one day when Del is walking to town to see if the scholarship marks have been posted, the real Bobby Sheriff, who has spent time in an asylum, invites her on to the verandah to share some cake he has baked.

Del becomes acutely aware of the limitations of the novel she is writing. "What happened to Bobby Sherriff when he had to stop baking cakes and go back to the Asylum? Such questions persist, in spite of novels. It is a shock when you have dealt so cunningly, powerfully, with reality, to come back and find it still there."

I think I really understood the Epilogue, perhaps for the first time, when I read it again as I wrote this book. When I first read *Lives* I didn't know what to make of it. It still comes as something of a shock, it pulls you up short, and seems almost to be outside the novel itself, after the narrative that brings you to this point has ended. It seems to me that in the Epilogue my mother is looking at what she really wants to do as an artist. She is saying here that there is no need to elaborate and embellish; people's lives are interesting enough if you can only capture them the way they really are. "People's lives, in Jubilee as elsewhere, were dull, simple, amazing and unfathomable – deep caves lined with kitchen linoleum."

Perhaps most of us are able to live with these tremendous

gaps about who people are and what their lives are like. We pick up on all the things like body language, and tone of voice, and how words are spoken, but the information mostly flows over us without really registering. We affix a few adjectives to a person and we move on. My mother can't do this. She always has to fill in the gaps, in the same way my son fills in the gaps about the physical world. He tries to get a picture in his mind of how the physical world fits together, how sound waves travel, what a black hole is, announcing at the breakfast table, "So time must have a beginning." This is how my mother treats people's lives. Recently she surprised me by saying that she "didn't have a self," that she was always "leapfrogging over herself" with her writing. I am beginning to understand what she meant.

LAST YEAR OF THE MARRIAGE

In the year after *Lives of Girls and Women* was published, and won the Canadian Booksellers Association International Book Year Award in 1972, my parents were being invited out all the time. Doors opened, people were paying attention to my mother who never had before, so my parents were leading a busy social life. But it was an awful year for them, that last year they were together. By this time my mother knew she had to get out of her marriage, and my father didn't want her to leave. She was just over forty, and had been married for twenty years. Many of their friends decided to break up their marriages at about this time. It was as if there was some centrifugal force at work in the culture, splitting families asunder, scattering children like leaves. The generation who had married in the fifties now had children who were almost grown up; they still had a chance to make up for what they had missed out on in their twenties. (It is easy to forget how young they were when they got married and had children. By contrast, I married at thirty-six and had one child at thirty-seven and another at forty-two.) A popular book at the time was called *Open Marriage*. The couple who wrote it split up when the open marriage idea didn't work; enterprisingly, they then produced another book called *Shifting Gears*. In this atmosphere it was no surprise that books like *The Joy of Sex* and *The Sensuous Woman* were all the rage.

She made the break gradually, first moving to an apartment over on Oak Bay Avenue, a few blocks away, and coming over to the house so she would be there when Andrea, who was now in grade one, got home from school, then leaving the house again after dinner. I was in my first year at the University of Victoria, taking a full slate of liberal arts courses: Art History, Classics, English, History, and Anthropology. I was still living at home and somehow everything was falling apart for me, too. I would mope around the house and follow my mother from room to room like a small child, pulled by an invisible cord. I would actually get short of breath when she left the room; she seemed to be avoiding me. In my classes I did not talk to anybody. If I knew I had to give an oral presentation in class, I would feel sick for weeks beforehand. Everyone else seemed to know people except me.

By this time my father was hardly speaking to me. As far as he was concerned, I was "an unpaying guest living in his house." As far as I was concerned, he was the MCP. My attitude towards him was increasingly flippant and mocking. I remember mouthing off to him after coming back from a trip to Vancouver, emboldened because I had been smoking a joint before I got home. He knocked me onto the floor on that occasion, the only time he ever did anything like that, and I can still see the look of helpless, animal rage in his eyes as I lay on my back. He was furious because my friends and I had to be put up at Children's Aid in downtown Vancouver when my friend's mysterious uncle – the one we were to stay with – did not materialize, and the city's "hippie crash pads" were all full.

I must have talked to my mother about how unhappy I was because she recommended that I make an appointment with the psychiatrist one of her friends was seeing. That friend had been advised to buy up cheap dishes and smash them against the wall in her basement as part of her therapy, as a way of working out her anger over the break-up of her marriage. The psychiatrist, I remember, had curly brown hair and a pink, babyish face. He would escort me into a little room off his office where there were some pillows and a plastic bat. I was to pound the pillows with the bat and express my rage. I felt silly doing this, and flailed around self-consciously, making unconvincing noises. I took this as a failure, a sign of how repressed and inhibited I must be. At other times we talked in his office – though it seemed to me he did most of the talking, recounting at length his problems getting through medical school because he had never learned to read properly. I don't know how we got onto the topic, but once he told me about how having a really good orgasm made his toes tingle. The thought of the psychiatrist having any kind of orgasm, good or otherwise, was not something I wanted to contemplate.

SOMETHING I'VE BEEN MEANING TO TELL YOU

After *Lives of Girls and Women* it took my mother a while to get down to the business of writing again, but by the

winter of 1973, the last year she would be with my father, she
was working steadily. She said there was something apprentice-
like about these new stories she was writing, that she was
"working from a shallower vein." What she meant was that
some of the stories in this collection were exercises, written to
see if she could pull something off, rather than the "breakthrough" stories like "The Peace of Utrecht" or, later, "Royal
Beatings," which used personal material in new ways. "The
Found Boat" was one such story; "Marrakesh" was another.
Stories she didn't think worked all that well were "The
Executioners" and "Walking on Water." Two of the stories
were condensed from novels she had worked on. "How I Met
My Husband" came from a novel she had started in West
Vancouver and which had to be aborted when her in-laws
came to stay for a month in the summer. The other was the
title story, "Something I've Been Meaning to Tell You," which
appears to have the span and breadth of a novel, because it was
in fact taken from a novel. Two of the stories are quite autobiographical, drawing on the childhood material she used in
Dance of the Happy Shades. These are "Winter Wind," a story
based on her grandmother and Aunt Maud, and "The Ottawa
Valley," the last story she wrote for the collection when she was
already living in London, a more autobiographical account of
her mother's illness than any other story.

Another autobiographical story composed in this period
was "Home," in which my grandfather and his second wife Etta
figure as characters. My mother did not want it to be included
in the collection, partly because of its autobiographical nature.
(It was published in *Best Canadian Stories*, 1974.) In this story
she used author intrusion, talking to the reader about the
writing process in the story itself, which she considered a

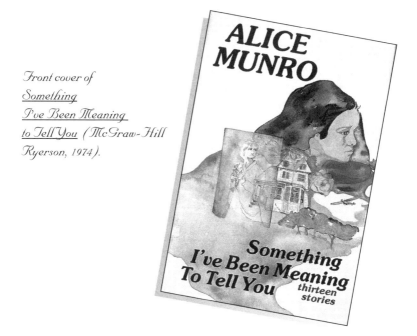

Front cover of
Something
I've Been Meaning
to Tell You (McGraw-Hill
Ryerson, 1974).

trendy literary device at that time, but used it just to prove she could write that kind of story. "Too slow as usual, all that approach with the three buses and then the house, too much house with the wallpaper and plastic chair cushions kind of thing, hardly anything yet about the people in it." In the character of Irlma she was obviously struggling with her new step-mother. "I feel guilty about her, what I am doing to her. Is this vengeful reporting, in spite of accuracy?" In the story Irlma launches into graphic detail about the bowel movements of her sick dog. I always had the feeling that my mother wanted to like Etta but couldn't, that it was an effort for her to be around Etta. It was easier for me and Jenny to like her, to accept her on her own terms. Flo in *Who Do You Think You Are?* reminded me a little of Etta.

While she was labouring on these stories in that upstairs

laundry room in the house on Rockland Avenue, I was traipsing around Europe with a girlfriend, hitchhiking, staying at youth hostels or grotty hippie crash pads, taking the "magic bus" from Athens to Amsterdam, visiting an exhausting succession of museums, art galleries, and cathedrals along the way. In "Tell Me Yes or No" (*Something*) she was writing about how different her own youth had been. "At the age when young girls nowadays are growing their hair to their waists, traveling through Afghanistan, moving – it seems to me – as smoothly as eels among their varied and innocent and transitory loves, I was sleepily rinsing diapers, clad in a red corduroy dressing gown; . . . I was pushing a baby carriage or a stroller." It is true I did all these things, but I was not really carefree the way she imagined I was. Nor were the "varied and transitory" loves all so innocent.

LEAVING

She told me the house seemed empty that final winter when I was away, that a sense of ending was in the air. In a letter that must have reached me somewhere in my travels, written in February, she filled me in on all the news. She had taken Jenny on a spur-of-the-moment bus trip to Palm Springs because the schools were on strike for four weeks. Andrea was getting very grown-up. "Yesterday she said, 'I don't want to grow up because then I'll have to get old and die.' 'Everybody dies,' said Jenny. 'I know,' said Andy. 'That's what I don't like about living. Dying.'" She informed me that she didn't get the job in Fredericton she had applied for – "Imagine, they didn't want me!" – but she did have a position at the University of Notre Dame in the town of

Nelson, British Columbia, teaching creative writing for the summer term.

When my mother did make the final break later that year, it was to go first to the teaching job in Nelson then on to a position she had been offered as writer-in-residence at the University of Western Ontario. She took Jenny and Andrea with her, and I stayed behind to work at Munro's and continue my university education. By then things were very bitter. Jenny remembers telling our father that she didn't know whether she should go to London or stay in Victoria. He told her to go with her mother.

Taking two trunks stuffed with letters, photographs, and memorabilia, and a verbal promise from my father that he would help pay for Andrea's education, my mother left the marriage for the last time.

CHAPTER 11

"So What Do You Write?"

1973 –2000

NELSON

That summer, the summer of 1974, I joined my mother and my sisters in the furnished apartment high on a hill overlooking Kootenay Lake. A description of what it was like living there can be found in the story "Providence" (*Who?*). The apartment building wrapped around a central courtyard and one morning I looked across into the window of the apartment across the courtyard and saw the feet. There were two pairs of feet, one facing up, the other facing down. The feet were jiggling. I called Jenny, and together we watched the feet.

Through Manpower, the government employment agency, I got myself a job as a roofer. My job was to dip a bucket in a vat of boiling hot tar and haul on a rope to hoist the bucket up to the roof. There were no safety standards and no protective clothing, not even gloves. After a few days of this I got another job working for the Department of Highways (Department of Holidays), raking rocks for the landscaping project around the new highway not far outside of town. We started at five in the morning just as the sun was coming up. I wore a halter top, cut-offs, and steel-capped boots. I had never done that kind of steady physical work before and I found it satisfying. It allowed my mind to range freely, mostly to think about the men I was meeting at the pub up at the college, where a few of us would congregate and drink beer in the evenings. There was John, with black hair falling to his shoulders and aviator glasses that gave him an intellectual look, and Ed, with hair to his waist – we called him "li'l Ed" – and Michael. I liked Michael the best, but he soon began showing up with his live-in girlfriend, a pretty dark-haired girl with eyebrows plucked pencil thin. We listened to John Denver's "Rocky Mountain High" and Seals and Crofts's "Diamond Girl," and once we went to a club downtown to hear the Slocan Valley's most famous band, Brain Damage. The back-to-the-land movement was still going full tilt and there was a large hippie community living in the Valley.

Jenny and I were sunning ourselves on the beach one afternoon when John came up to us, carrying a copy of James Joyce's *Ulysses*, and sat down on our blanket. I allowed him to put suntan lotion on my back and legs and made a great show of giggling and kicking as his hands travelled higher and higher up my legs. Jenny was there too, deeply disappointed by my behaviour. She let me know this later. Besides being in the creative writing class, John was president of the Student Council, a big wheel on campus. My mother never told me at the time, but I found out later that he was very rude in her class and used to put his feet up on the table as an indication of disdain. Actually he was a fairly nasty character. Once when I was visiting him at the tiny house he lived in, my mother dropped in for a visit; afterwards he chided me, "You

didn't say a single word. I was so disappointed in you." With all
the bright, witty, boisterous talk going on I could not, could
not speak. Even when we were alone together, I could not speak
to John either. We were riding the bus together one day when,
after a long silence, I said: "So what do you think of the
Watergate hearings?"

By the end of the summer I was living with John. I decided
to switch to the University of British Columbia in Vancouver,
rather than go back to UVic, so I would be close enough to visit
him on weekends. But Vancouver was hardly next door to
Nelson. On Fridays after my classes, I would go down to the
bus depot downtown with a bottle of ouzo stashed in my bag
(ouzo was John's favourite drink) and set off into the night
staring at my own reflection in the window for the twelve-hour
bus ride. I would have breakfast in Osoyoos, finally taking a cab
and crawling into his bed in the morning. All that autumn, I'd
call him from the hall outside the room I rented and the phone
would ring and ring and ring. If he did answer he sounded curt
and angry, but I still wasn't getting it.

When I was going through all this, my mother wrote to me.
"The point is you have to withdraw attention – either as a
tactic or to save yourself. As long as you're there, suffering and
bitching, but there, hung up on him, the situation is not going
to change. Being in love that way just isn't good, there must be
a better, self-sufficient way to love. (I am preaching to myself as
well as you.) Get so you don't need him. Work at it. Then of
course he may come back all humble and interested (that happened to me with . . .). Women like us have got to get away
from emotional dependency or life is just one dreary man-
made seesaw. Take this to heart."

VICTORIA, SEPTEMBER 1999

My mother, my sister Jenny, and I and are staying at the Crystal Court Motel in downtown Victoria, in the heart of the tourist district, getting ready to attend my sister Andrea's wedding reception. After working for my father at Munro's for several years (the store is now located in a beautiful neo-classical building, Victoria's old Royal Bank, on Government Street), Andrea has moved to Calgary with Todd, a theatre technical director, and has just gotten married. Like me, Andrea is a writer. She has published articles, a short story, and most recently had a play of hers, *The Sky Is Falling*, produced in Calgary. This day it happens to be my birthday as well, and Andrea has given me a copy of a book on meditation, *Wherever You Go, There You Are.* Jenny has come out from Toronto, where she is preparing for her second art show, bringing me a sarong splashed with orange and purple. In the morning Jenny and I get up early and look out the window to the Crystal Gardens across the street and the Empress Hotel beyond. There is a brightness in the air you do not see anywhere else; the sun rises and the buildings are gilded, the sky impossibly blue. We decide to walk through Beacon Hill Park, trailing through bleached summer grass, past the Garry oaks, and the field where my brother-in-law plays cricket like his great-grandfather before him, and come at last to the little playground on Cook Street where we used to play, where Jenny cut her leg open on the wooden swing. Her friend Bev ran from the scene to our house yelling, "Mrs. Munro, Mrs. Munro, Jenny cut her leg off! Jenny cut her leg off!" Robert Weaver was visiting her at the time. I wonder if the swing is still there with the bloodstain still in it, but of course it isn't, it's all new playground equipment now.

We wander up Cook Street in a nostalgic mood, towards the ocean past the stone house with its verandah and stained-glass windows. "Do you remember the cats and how they smelled?" asks Jenny. I remember the cats but not the smell. I point out the quaint white house where an old couple named the Shaws once lived. The chestnut trees on the boulevard are unchanged, leaves edged with brown and gold the way they were that first fall after we moved here. We stop in front of the house we lived in, not much changed since then either, the grey stucco now taupe, with artful arbours and bamboo screens added for shade and privacy. When we come back to the motel, Audrey Thomas has arrived. She is sitting at the little table in the kitchenette painting her fingernails green in preparation for the event.

Later, my mother and I are alone, and I'm standing in front of the mirror of a suite that hasn't changed since the fifties: coved ceilings, a neat kitchenette, two leather armchairs. We love staying here; together we imagine how we could redecorate, repainting the dingy-looking walls, replacing the carpet, arranging plants and cushions. "It has everything you need," she says, and we are both drawn into the fantasy of a life without housework, for me a life without children, a life without encumbrances. "You could have people over to dinner," she says, pointing to the dinette suite, and we imagine this pared-down life focussed on work. My mother has never lived on her own, has never had quite enough uninterrupted time for writing; the one thing she has longed for is solitude.

MOVING TO LONDON

"She doesn't speak of leaving a husband of 20 years and a

12-room house in Victoria B.C. as though it was a cataclysmic experience. Nor does Alice speak of packing all the worldly possessions she wanted into two trunks and moving to London as though it was the decision of a newly-liberated woman. She talks about it as though she had done nothing very remarkable at all."

– from an interview with Joanna Beyersbergen in
The London Free Press, June 22, 1974

The closest she came to living on her own was in the fall of 1974, when she and my sisters moved to London, Ontario, where she had been offered a position as writer-in-residence at the University of Western Ontario. "Celebrated drop-out returns" read the headlines, somewhat unfairly, since she really did not have any choice but to drop out of university once the scholarship money ran out. At Western she wouldn't be teaching a class the way she had in Nelson. She and the head of the English department agreed that "creative writing could not be taught," but she was there to offer individual support. She was forty-three years old and she had just published *Something I've Been Meaning to Tell You*.

I would have been at UBC when she sent news of the place she and Jenny and Andrea hoped to live in. "We have found a terrific house – about 100 years old – 3 bedrooms – you must come when term's over. $190 a month. But the owners are very 'particular.' We are invited to a brunch this morning to see how we all behave. Oh, I really love it. Red carpet on the stairs, white walls and woodwork – the danger with old houses is that somebody will have 'modernized' it, meaning flowered paper & lime green colour scheme . . . I quit my job. Nothing like increasing expenses & cutting out steady income at the same time. I feel it was the right thing to do. I just have to cut down the strain somewhere."

She meant the job she had had teaching at York University in Toronto. She had just notified the English department there that she would not be returning to teach creative writing in the spring semester, as she had in the fall, when she had to make a four-hour commute to Toronto twice a week. She found teaching really difficult.

Despite my mother's contention that she was "mining a shallower vein" with her new stories, the reviews for *Something* were unanimously favourable. Critics welcomed those new stories that branched off from the young-girl-growing-up-in-rural-Ontario material, and explored the darker, more ambiguous terrain of adult lives. In the words of one reviewer, "her talents were transportable." The two stories most often singled out for praise were "Material" and "Memorial" (incidentally the two stories she considers the best in that collection). "Material" looks at the moral obligations of a writer from the point of view of his wife, who has to acknowledge that for all his posturing and affectation, and his shabby treatment of their downstairs neighbour, he has created something of lasting value in his art. "Memorial" is a complex look at a family who have dealt with a son's death in a controlled, almost fashionable manner, which is morally unacceptable to the narrator.

I think it's true that we all read, to some extent, in order to learn about life. It is through reading stories like these that I came to be ever more wary of the facades people erect for themselves, like Hugo with his claims about being a logger – and wary, too, of the falseness that can come with any kind of orthodoxy, not just traditional orthodoxy, but the liberal, unconventional orthodoxy of the family in "Memorial." People who were Unitarians, like my parents' friends.

Journalists who interviewed this "blue-jeaned, make-upless" woman when she came back to London asked the most personal, even intimate, questions. What was she attracted to in a man? How did her daughters feel about her not being a "normal" mother? How had they been affected by the women's liberation movement? And she answered all the questions candidly and thoughtfully. It seems to me that in those times journalists were not trying to extract celebrity gossip the way they do now; they were genuinely curious to find out how others were finding their way in a world where the old signposts were being torn down.

In Canada in the mid-seventies there was this surge of women authors coming to the fore, new stars like Marian Engel and Audrey Thomas, and the emerging triumvirate of Margaret Atwood, Margaret Laurence, and my mother, who were cracking the shell of the female experience wide open. It was all new and exciting, and of course the fiction tied in with the women's movement. Fifty years before, Virginia Woolf had admitted that she hadn't been able to write about a woman's experience in the body, that perhaps no woman had been able to do that, and now that was exactly what these women were doing.

After that year in Vancouver – post-John – I moved back to Victoria. I began my third year of university as an English major at UVic while once again working part-time at Munro's. By then I had acquired a new boyfriend, Rob, and we were living together. The next summer we drove across the country in his Ford van to visit my mother and my sisters in London. Gerry Fremlin had come on the scene by then. He had looked her up at Western, ostensibly with a manuscript to show her, and they drank three martinis each at the Faculty Club lounge. After working as a geographer in Ottawa editing *The National Atlas of Canada,* he had retired early, and returned to his family home in Clinton to look after his mother, who was in her eighties. My mother was soon living there as well.

That summer in London was a wild time; there were parties, lots of drinking. "Auntie Marg," my father's youngest sister, who had been living in London and raising a family all these years, became friends with my mother. She had left her marriage and a house in the suburbs and was going back to school. A kind of adolescent hilarity prevailed whenever Rob and I visited. Andrea had gone to a school I knew only by the name of "the free school," which I understand was shaky on academic instruction but great on creative self-expression. Jenny had moved to Montreal with a friend, and Rob and I visited her there that summer in her apartment near St. Urbain Street. She got a job in a textile factory and took art courses at McGill before returning to London and taking art at Beal Technical College.

My father had a new woman in his life, Victoria artist Carole Sabiston, whom he married in the "chapel" at Rockland after my parents' divorce came through. One of the first things Carole did after moving into the house with her ten-year-old son Andrew was to put straw hats on the busts of Beethoven and Bach that sat on top of the piano. Now that my father was with Carole it was agreed that Andrea would spend the school year with them and the summers with my mother and Gerry in Clinton. Unlike me, she attended private schools, first Norfolk House and then St. Michael's University School, and took up horseback riding. I visited the Rockland house fairly frequently, and gradually was reconciled with my father, so that now we are good friends.

I dropped out of university near the beginning of my fourth

year. I was taking a course in French literature and I found out that it wouldn't do for my French requirement; I needed a course in conversational French, and I could not bear the thought of having to speak in French. That was one problem. The other problem had to do with my seminar course in contemporary British literature. I remember we were studying D.H. Lawrence's novel *The Rainbow* and in every class I would try to join in the discussion. Growing hot and sweaty, my heart pounding, I would be thinking, "I'll say something now, I'll just get this sentence ready in my head first, oh, now it's too late, the discussion has moved on, I can't say it now." It was those Laidlaw genes. I'd stagger out of the class afterwards all wobbly in the knees, time after time, without having contributed anything at all.

Some time around the beginning of November I just stopped going to classes and dropped out of sight (I'm thinking of my grandfather leaving school), working full-time at Munro's. Soon I was managing the new branch store a few blocks away at a place called Market Square; my father made sure everyone knew I got the job because I had the most seniority, not because I was his daughter. It was in the old part of town near Chinatown where original warehouses had been converted into stores and restaurants. After another year and a half I decided I'd had enough of Munro's, too, even though as store manager I got to do all the ordering, as well as receiving ten per cent of the profits on top of my regular salary. Even though I wasn't working directly with him any more, the terrible tension between my father and myself had hardly diminished. Naturally, he'd resented Jenny and me calling him the MCP and being cast as the ogre, while my mother got off scot-free. He even saw me as being partly responsible for the break-up of his marriage. Feeling as he did, that I was "agin him," what point was there in trying to patch things up? But when I told him I was leaving – I had decided to move to Toronto – he did not take it well, even though he'd told me that as a Munro's employee, "You're not the best, but you're not the worst."

And so I moved to Toronto, gravitating towards my mother's part of the country, without giving much thought to what I would do there. Almost right away I landed a job as a clerk in a library (Locke library in North Toronto) and found a tiny apartment in the Annex neighbourhood, near downtown. Locke library was called the punishment branch because no one wanted to work there. That must have been why there was an opening. I hated not being able to answer questions about books because I was only a clerk, and I tidied the shelves and stamped out books in a sullen mood that did not go unobserved by the head librarian, Miss McNeil, who held meetings to discuss "my attitude" in her office. After a year or so I escaped and began working at the SCM Book Room in the Rochdale College building on Bloor Street, running the mail-order department. The building was close to being a ruin in those days, almost completely empty after being trashed by student radicals in the sixties. Jenny came to Toronto and we lived together briefly before she went off to Trent University in Peterborough, Ontario, where she lasted a year before calling it quits.

Periodically I met my mother in the Irish pub at the corner of Yonge and Bloor Street or at our favourite restaurant, The Copenhagen Room, or went up to Clinton on weekends, where she and Gerry were living in the white Victorian gingerbread house on the outskirts of town where Gerry had grown up.

WHO DO YOU THINK YOU ARE?

I n the years following the publication of *Something I've Been Meaning to Tell You*, when I was living in Toronto, my mother's career was gathering momentum. In 1978 she wrote the script for "1847," a moving documentary about the Irish coming to Canada, as part of CBC Television's *Newcomer* series. That same year her fourth book, *Who Do You Think You Are?*, was published by Macmillan with her new editor, Doug Gibson (and published as *The Beggar Maid* in the American edition because it was thought that American readers wouldn't under-stand the implications of the original title), to national and international acclaim. Subtitled *Stories of Flo and Rose*, it was another collection of interrelated stories as *Lives* had been, drawing on the mother/daughter theme (I always saw Etta as Flo). It followed Rose's adventures as a young girl, a wife, a

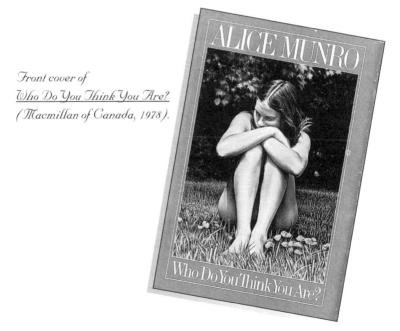

Front cover of
Who Do You Think You Are?
(Macmillan of Canada, 1978).

mother, and eventually a divorced woman, and had a darker, more mature vision than the earlier book. Much was made in literary circles of my mother's last-minute decision to have the stories, which were originally about two women, Janet and Rose, changed so they were all about Rose, and how she paid for these very late changes out of her own pocket. For this collection, she won her second Governor General's Award in 1978. By this time she was publishing stories in *The New Yorker* regularly, with the help of her American agent, Virginia Barber. She made it onto *The New York Times*'s bestseller list. From then on her writing life began to settle into a predictable pattern: stories published in *The New Yorker* at regular intervals, a collection every four years or so followed by the usual accolades, ecstatic reviews, large sales, and a succession of honours and prizes. And she was making money.

SO WHAT DO YOU WRITE?

At the time *Who Do You Think You Are?* came out in 1978, I had fallen in with some literary types in Toronto. I remember being in a bar once with a group of writers. We were all drinking beer and people were bringing out poems and passing them around. Then the guy next to me turned around and asked, "So what do you write?" Probably he was just being politely conversational, but at the time I thought he was mocking me because I was Alice Munro's daughter, and I was stung. I managed to mumble something about "Well, nothing really," before slinking off to the washroom, hiding in a cubicle, and weeping inconsolably. After some time, Jocelyn

Laurence (who was writing book reviews for *The Globe and Mail* and had even interviewed my mother, very shrewdly noting her shaking hands) came to rescue me. As Margaret Laurence's daughter she understood some of my problem. But she had a successful career of her own. What was wrong with me? Why couldn't I be a writer?

VANCOUVER

G radually things got better for me. By the time *The Moons of Jupiter* came out in 1982 I was in Vancouver and had gone back to finish my English degree at UBC, studiously avoiding courses in Canadian Literature, of course, in case the instructor found out WHO I WAS and made me into a public

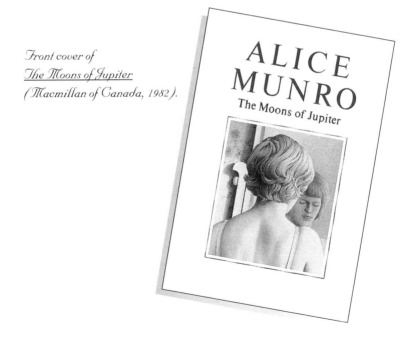

Front cover of
The Moons of Jupiter
(Macmillan of Canada, 1982).

spectacle. After a couple of aimless years working in dead-end jobs and living in basement suites, I returned to school, to Simon Fraser University this time, on Burnaby Mountain, east of the city, and acquired a teaching certificate. I couldn't really imagine myself teaching in a classroom, and there were no jobs anyway at that time, but I did manage to get work as a tutor, teaching English as a Second Language to the sons and daughters of Asian immigrants in their luxury homes in Kerrisdale. I had a nice boyfriend, a physicist at UBC's TRIUMF facility. Eventually I became a book reviewer for *The Vancouver Sun*, writing in the morning, driving from one student to the next from four until eight or so at night. I left the nice boyfriend, moved to another basement suite in Kitsilano (the district that is the setting for "Cortes Island" in *The Love of a Good Woman*), and continued writing and tutoring, at last getting my name onto the substitute-teacher list in Vancouver. I even worked at the Carnegie library downtown, in the heart of the notorious downtown east side, on Friday and Saturday nights, so I would have enough cash. This was about the time *The Progress of Love* came out in 1986. I discarded the subbing, the tutoring, and the library job in an instant when I finally landed a "real job" as a researcher for DIAND (the Department of Indian Affairs and Northern Development) with my own office in the Royal Bank office tower downtown and a view looking out over Stanley Park. I rode the elevator in my boxy eighties suit with the shoulder pads, clutching my briefcase self-importantly, swinging my freshly highlighted hair.

During all this time, the years in Toronto and Vancouver, my mother and I got together at various restaurants or drinking establishments. More than almost anything else in my life I looked forward to those meetings alone with her – when we

Front cover of
The Progress of Love
(Douglas Gibson Books/
McClelland and Stewart, 1986).

were with anyone else there was an air of tact and restraint, and I couldn't really have the kind of high-voltage exchange with her I wanted to have. I'd see her coming up the street in her leather pants, maybe some tight turtleneck, something dramatic, no grey showing in her hair because she used a product called Happiness ("I really have found happiness" she used to joke), and I'd be in a state of breathless anticipation. Our conversations were intense, intimate, far-ranging. We shared everything, our love lives, our friendships, the books we were reading, the movies we'd seen, clothes, hair, face lifts, literary gossip, witnesses to the follies, vanities, and self-deceptions of other people's lives. There was always a sense of excitement; it was as if we were trying to get to some perspective, some stance, where we could see everything as it truly was. Whether we were enjoying a drink in the old Sylvia Hotel in Vancouver's west end, or having souvlaki and a carafe of Greek wine on Robson Street, or savouring the open-faced smoked salmon sandwiches at Toronto's Copenhagen Room, I felt with her that I could get places – of insight, and awareness, and wonder – that I could reach with no one else.

Yet there was something a little shameful about it, as if for her I wanted to be the perfect audience and the ideal friend, the one who stayed behind and waited like a proud parent while she went out into the front lines, to readings and book signings, interviews and awards ceremonies, and came back to tell me all about it. She had this illustrious career, and a life full of recognition, fame, travel, money, and a satisfying relationship, while I had . . . well, my basement suite, my tutoring, my three close friends. It wasn't my relationship *with* her that was the problem. It was my relationship *to* her, it was being "Alice Munro's daughter." It was as if she had all the talent, the vivacity, the humour, *all the words*, while I had . . . nothing at all.

THE SUBLIME ALICE

The other day a friend of mine told me that Alice had been described on CBC Radio as "the best short-story writer in the western world." Well, why not? Why not just say the best in the universe and get it over with? I never know how to respond when people tell me these things. I try to assume an air of gracious surprise. I hate the idea that the offspring of famous and talented parents are somehow damaged, victims even, just because their mother or father happens to be unusually successful. Women, especially, feel guilty when their daughters are made aware of their triumphs, as if they expect to have to pay a price, to make it up to them. "Well, isn't that wonderful?" I say, swallowing an unmistakable taste of chagrin. What else can I do? After all, it's true what everyone is saying. I agree with them. Did I know *Open Secrets* won the W.H. Smith Award for the best book in Britain that year? "Oh yes, I heard. Isn't it marvellous?" And how about *The Love of a Good Woman* winning the National Book Critics Circle Prize as the best fiction book of the year in the U.S.A.? "Wonderful, isn't it?" Did I know she'd won the Molson Prize, the Giller, the Governor General's Award *for the third time*? I act as if nothing could make me happier. Moping or sulking, acting churlish, would hardly seem attractive, would it? But is my whole life to be built around living vicariously through my mother? There is something so out-of-proportion about having *Alice Munro* as my mother. To

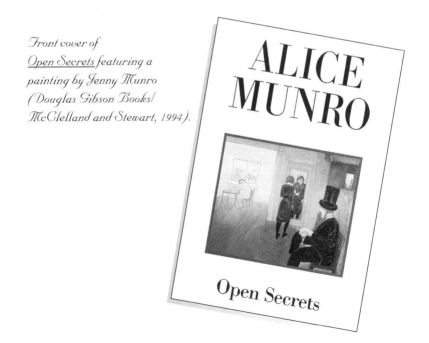

Front cover of Open Secrets featuring a painting by Jenny Munro (Douglas Gibson Books/ McClelland and Stewart, 1994).

hear these things is the psychological equivalent of looking out over the Grand Canyon. You lose all perspective.

Now when I read a review of a collection of Canadian short stories, I am just waiting for the "A-word." The writer is usually not as good as my mother, may not have the authenticity, or perhaps reminds us of her. I saw one reference recently to a young woman being hailed as the "new Alice Munro," while another headline claims to have discovered "Russia's Alice Munro." Short-story writing, in Canada at least, seems almost to be defined in terms of her work. Her take on small-town life seems embedded in the Canadian psyche. For example, one commentator on CBC Radio was talking about the pros and cons of living in a small town, and said something like, "Oh, I don't know if it would be so great. I've read my Alice Munro." And I can't begin to count the number of women who have told me what a tremendous impact reading *Lives of Girls and Women* had on them as young women in the seventies. She is the gold standard by which everything else is measured, to whom everyone else is compared. And I can understand why. I do not disagree. It's just that it makes her into an icon and I don't suppose anyone wants their mother, or their father for that matter, to become an icon. What is there to do with an icon besides worshipping it, or ignoring it, or smashing it to pieces?

A few years back, when I was trying to write fiction, I asked a writer friend of mine, someone from my writers' group, to look at a story I had written. He sat down at my kitchen table and started going over the manuscript with me paragraph by paragraph. "What does this mean? And this line doesn't work here. I would change the ending if I were you." The pages in front of me were covered in red ink, and beginning to blur because, horror of horrors, my eyes were filling with tears. I concentrated all my efforts on not letting those tears spill over, and heard him out without breaking down. When he was leaving he left me a copy of a poem he had written; it was dedicated to my mother and it contained a reference to the way she described the quality of light in Victoria. Would I be kind enough to give it to her?

On another occasion, when I was trying to write historical pieces for a B.C. magazine, I was telling a friend about an article I was doing on the brideships that came to Victoria in the nineteenth century. My mother happened to be visiting at the time and my friend turned to her and said, "Oh Alice, you should be the one writing this. Imagine what *you* could do with it." As it turned out, the article I wrote was fairly dull.

People have introduced me simply as Alice Munro's daughter, or sometimes, overcome by the proximity to fame, as Alice Munro. How can one not feel overshadowed? Sometimes people gush, "Oh, your mother is sooo beautiful." More often they are discreet. I happen to know that in several of the stores my mother and I frequent when she comes over to Powell River, the women working there are great fans of hers. But they exercise admirable restraint as my mother and I exclaim over dresses and scarves and tablecloths and Turkish carpets. "This one might work for you," says one, holding up a white blouse. Many of my friends name my mother as their favourite author, among them the artist/carpenter who has just finished some renovations on our house, and the daycare worker who looked after Thomas at the Busy Bee Daycare while I was writing; the retired neighbour across the street, who borrowed my copy of *The Love of a Good Woman*, and the boy next door who read "Images" in his English class, the administrative secretary at the School Board Office who has her stories on tape, even my

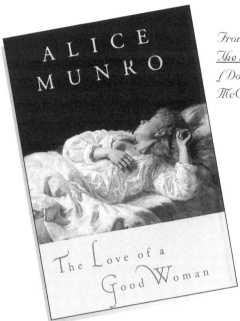

Front cover of
The Love of a Good Woman
(Douglas Gibson Books/
McClelland and Stewart, 1998).

dental hygienist, who told me about a dream she had after reading "My Mother's Dream."

I read once that when a certain group of well-known Canadian women writers got together to discuss literature, they referred to my mother as "The Sublime Alice." That really put the cap on it.

My mother does not invite all the adulation and tributes. For instance, she is not the kind of person who cares about what table she gets in a restaurant. She does not enjoy being recognized in public, though fortunately that happens only rarely. But what she likes least, of course, is all the baggage that comes with fame, all the requests for appearances, the manuscripts that are sent to her, the letters of reference, the book blurbs to write, the committees to be on, the good works to be done. She tries to turn them all down, politely explaining that she needs time to write. She said something interesting about the dangers of being a famous person; she said the danger was not that she would do badly in all the interviews and performances, what was distressing was how easy it was to become good at it, to become glib, and to cease to have any authentic feeling to write about.

My mother can get very annoyed by the way fame distracts her from her writing time. Once when she received an award in the mail (I forget which one) all she could think of was how the little styrofoam balls packed in with the award had spilled onto the floor, making a big mess she would have to clean up. The truth is, she has given her life to writing those stories, and she wants to concentrate all her energy on doing that. That is why she has never even kept a journal and has produced only a handful of non-fiction pieces. And that is why she has not been very involved with the Writers' Union, or PEN International, or

Canadian Gothic.
My mother and Gerry
in Clinton, 1990.

any literary society, however worthy. With rare exceptions, such as her work on the Giller Prize jury and as a member of the editorial board of the New Canadian Library, her energy is limited to doing this one thing.

POWELL RIVER

I am lying on the couch looking up at the rippling patterns of light on the ceiling, reflections off the waves from the sea visible outside the window. It is September but every day has been hot and sunny, hot enough for us to swim in the ocean, easing ourselves in off the rocks at high tide, swimming out to the "alligator rock" we can stand on. Right now, the heat and the ripples of light are making me feel sick. I'm six weeks pregnant, and I'm thinking the term "morning sickness" must have been invented by a man. What I've been feeling since the honeymoon is like a constant seasickness; this cottage by the sea is like a ship in a rolling swell.

The house on Tweedsmuir Avenue in Powell River, 1991.

Powell River is not really on an island, but it feels like an island because you can only get here by taking a ferry from Vancouver Island or Vancouver, or by plane. I used to fly up here when Monty and I were courting. I'd met him through a mutual friend in Vancouver, intrigued when she told me his idea of the perfect day would be to read *The New York Times* newspaper from cover to cover. We got together on a few occasions, but for me nothing really clicked until I saw him in church at a friend's wedding. He was a few pews ahead of me, sitting up straight between his mother and father: tall, lanky, bespectacled. "Ah, there's a confirmed bachelor," I thought to myself. On the church steps after the ceremony I came up to him. "Sheila," he said, giving me a hug. After that we went off to the English pub at Oak Bay Beach Hotel, and then on to the wedding reception.

Soon I was flying on weekends up to Powell River, where he had a teaching job. From the plane I could look down

*My mother and Monty at our wedding in 1990,
with my father framed between them.*

upon the string of tiny islands along the coast, sandy coves, lighthouses, woods, outcroppings of glacial rock, and then the ribbon of sand and the neat row of roofs and squares of lawn of the waterfront properties stretching along the highway, then the town itself, on a hillside facing west where you can look out over Texada and Harwood islands to the mountains of Vancouver Island and the Comox Glacier. As we bank and turn in towards the airport I can see the pulp-and-paper mill clinging to the edge of the water at the northern end of the town, and the streets and houses of the original company townsite, built in about 1911. At night the mill is lit up like one of those monstrous Alaska-bound cruise ships that glide by silently on summer evenings with their dazzling lights, floating palaces, or more likely floating Vegases. Close up, in broad daylight, the cement structures and belching smoke-stacks of the mill are not so appealing; Blake's line about the "dark Satanic mills" becomes a mental tic whenever I drive by. Every once in a while, most often in summer, a sulphuric tang permeates the air of the town. "Eau de mill," we call it, those of us who live here.

During my pregnancy, I write archly to friends back in Vancouver about the "rustic paradise" we have found ourselves in, and mention the cedar-shake cottage, the stone fireplace, the two blue herons who inhabit our stretch of beach, the eagles, the beach encrusted with oysters and mussels and bar-nacles that crunch under your feet, even the purple starfish clinging to the undersides of the rocks. I sit on the deck and watch a steady parade of pleasure boats, tugs, and fishing rigs plying their way up and down Malaspina Strait. Or I might walk up to the little meadow surrounded by trees above the cottage and lie down in the long grass imagining how I will bring my baby up here for picnics. I didn't know there would be bugs, it would be too hot, there would never be time.

By Christmas I was "showing," and women everywhere were telling me their stories about being pregnant and giving birth. I had joined the club now. I was working a little as a substitute teacher, up until March, when I got to the "beached whale" stage. My baby boy was born at seven P.M. on April 24, after about twenty hours of "active" labour and four hours of "pushing." (I could have used some of that tincture of opium that my mother had.) I hadn't thought of boys' names because I was so sure I would have a girl and name her Clare, but we soon settled on James Montague, after my father and Monty's father.

EGMONT STREET

My mother is walking slowly up the hill in a black slouchy hat, black pants, looking down at the sidewalk until she looks up smiling, radiant in the midst of some private concentration, then comes up the walk to our stucco bungalow on Egmont Street, the house we bought when James was a year old. He is two now and she has come over on the ferry from her condominium in Comox, where she and Gerry spend the winter months (a happy coincidence, since she bought it before she ever knew that I would live in Powell River). Today she will be looking after James while I write. I might be working on a "gender-equity kit" or producing educational materials on the perils of drugs and alcohol use, or compiling a list of sexually transmitted diseases. Intermittently I do contract work for the local school district. Or it could be that I'm

James and my mother in 1991.

working on one of my "vignettes," writing exercises of five hundred words or so. The book I'm reading tells me to start with "I remember," or just describe what I see in front of me. "Keep the hand moving," the book advises. Don't worry about grammar or punctuation. I resurrect episodes from my past, or I might even describe what it's like walking down Marine Avenue in Powell River.

Today she takes James in the stroller to the playground down at Willingdon Beach. She is delighted to be able to do this for me, and delighted with James himself, taking an interest in him as an individual, in what he's thinking and feeling and imagining, that goes far beyond the usual grandmother-to-grandson relationship. She surprises me with how maternal and solicitous she is. She expresses a tender concern for us, for James when he had pneumonia, sensing that he needed to get to the doctor. For myself she expresses a rather geriatric maternity, telling me once that I needed to get to a doctor, commiserating with me over how hard it was to do what I was doing, mothering two rambunctious boys, "trying to write," running a household, resisting the demands of the community. The demands came from schools and organizations that can assume that a mother's time is more or less at others' disposal. It is only because of her example and encouragement that I was able to pay for daycare so that I could write, and turn down baking, crossing guard, head-lice check, driving – all those things we are called on to do, that eat into whatever free time we might have. She frequently exclaims over what a good mother I am, how patient I am, how much I play with James, and expresses regret over not having spent more time with me and my sisters when we were little.

My mother and James in the kitchen on Egmont Street.

There seems something ironic about this, *my mother* taking James for a walk so I can write. Secretly I feel like a fraud. I'm not a *real writer*. Yes, I've written book reviews, but everyone – especially reviewers – knows they don't really count. I submit a series of sketches about marriage and motherhood called "Diary of a Mad Housewife" to my local writers' group for everyone to critique. I make journal entries about how I must will myself into being a successful writer. I must submit ideas to magazines. I must be published.

An idea grows out of this. I am interested in women's lives, I am interested in social history, I am something of a feminist. I loved the book *Parallel Lives: Five Victorian Marriages* by Phyllis Rose, about the marriages of famous Victorians like Dickens and Ruskin, about what it was like for the wives. Why couldn't I do a book on the lives of pioneer women in British Columbia? I could have chapters on women from different classes, I could explore their marriages, motherhood, domestic life, the role of religion. I could write about my own life and compare it to theirs. I began to chat about my idea with friends and acquaintances, prattling on with enthusiasm, meeting with interest and approval. I was saying to them and to myself, "See, I am doing something with my life. I am someone."

I contact an editor and begin what she tells my mother is a "white hot" correspondence with her. I visit the Provincial Archives in Victoria and begin my research, reading the journals and letters of early women settlers who sailed around the Horn from England, poring over handwritten letters from relatives in England, written horizontally and then vertically over top in order to save paper. I read of broken engagements, marriages, the sudden deaths of children from cholera, of dances, and teaching Sunday School, of mysterious ailments, and sewing new dresses and bonnets. Trying to recover the past. Like Uncle Craig in *Lives of Girls and Women*. Like R.A. Laidlaw in Vancouver. Like my grandfather.

I had such a sense of purpose waving goodbye to Monty and James at the ferry dock, toting my briefcase off to the Archives in Victoria like the researcher I had recently been, and returning with my treasures, stacks of photocopies of letters and diaries I had discovered. Part of me knew it was a false enthusiasm, however, that I was talking too much about doing it and writing too little. I was trying to prove to myself, *See, I can do this. Aren't my ideas interesting?* Everyone was asking me about how the book was going. But when I sat down with all this material spread out before me, I hadn't a clue how to begin. The Emperor had no clothes. It was like the time we neighbourhood kids invited all the neighbours to our production of "Sleeping Beauty" and they started arriving and we hadn't rehearsed, nobody knew their lines, and we never got past the first scene with Sleeping Beauty as a baby and me as her mother. Time passed and I realized I was never going to get past chapter one. Gradually people stopped asking me how the book was going. A tactful silence ensued.

LIVES OF MOTHERS AND DAUGHTERS

In 1997, my mother asked me if I wanted to write her biography. By this time I was the mother of two sons. Thomas Guy was born in 1995, a month after my forty-second birthday. We had moved a few blocks up the hill to the kind of suburban home – with a deck above the carport and a family room downstairs – that I could never have imagined living in before I had children. I didn't have any strong reaction to my mother's idea at that time, so I let the matter drop. Then about six months later, I realized that I did want to write about her, but of course I was the wrong person to write a biography; I was much too close to her for that. What I wanted to do was to write a memoir about what it was like growing up as her daughter.

For years I had been writing vignettes about my own life, but I could never find any framework into which they would fit; they seemed to be going nowhere, and I was growing more and more frustrated. It occurred to me that perhaps I could use a memoir as a framework. And as for learning more about Alice Munro, I was in the unique position of being able to talk to her any time I wanted, about anything and everything under the sun. I was having conversations with her that other writers would kill for. Soon I started taping our conversations over lunch at The Old House Restaurant in Courtenay, and very quickly everything fell into place. I knew without a doubt that this was what I had to do. And in the months and years since then, for me everything has continued to fall into place, and I continue to feel this way.

My mother, Alice Munro, in my kitchen in 1994.

Recently I had a dream. In the dream I was riding along in a train with my mother. It was sort of a luxury train and we were sitting on red plush seats looking out at the scenery and I was enjoying the ride, but I realized that I had to get onto my own train. I knew my train was coming, but I didn't know if I was going to be able to get onto it. Then my train pulled alongside and we stopped and I had to get across some tracks to reach it but I had all this baggage with me, so my mother and I had to haul all these bags from her train to an open boxcar on mine. I didn't know if I'd get everything on before my train left. At the end of my dream I did get onto my train – but I don't know if it started moving or not. At least I hadn't missed it.

From top to bottom: Thomas, me, and James in Powell River, 2000.

ACKNOWLEDGEMENTS

I gratefully acknowledge the financial support of the Canada Council for the Arts for making it possible for me to write this book. I would like to thank my sisters, Jenny and Andrea, for reading the manuscript and offering suggestions, my father, Jim Munro, for his enthusiastic support and input, and for taking all those family photographs over the years. My thanks also go to Allan Brown, for his astute comments and unflagging support, to Carla Mobley and all the members of The Malaspina Writers' Association, and to my editor, Douglas Maitland Gibson, for his remarkable skill in "guiding me through the maze."

I am grateful to Daphne Cue, Douglas Spettigue, David Cook, and Gerald Fremlin for sharing their memories, to my aunt Sheila Laidlaw-Radford for allowing me to quote from her letters, and especially to Robert Weaver, who provided me with copies of his correspondence with my mother.

I was greatly aided in my research by the biography *A Double Life*, by Catherine Sheldrick Ross, and I am indebted to the many scholars and journalists who have written about my mother and her work over the years. I would like to thank J. Mac Jamieson for posting my grandfather's memoir, *Boyhood Summer 1912*, on the internet.

And to Monty, and our sons James and Thomas, my thanks for their patience and understanding.

Finally, I would like to thank my mother. This book could not have been written without her willingness to talk to me about her life and work with complete candour and honesty.

Sheila Munro
Powell River
January 2001

INDEX